Final Report

Circulation, thermohaline structure, and cross-shelf transport in the Alaskan Beaufort Sea

Principal Investigator: Thomas Weingartner
School of Fisheries and Ocean Sciences
University of Alaska
Fairbanks, AK 99775

May 2006

Table of Contents

List of Figures

List of Tables

Abstract

This project was undertaken to investigate the along-slope structure and variability in the circulation and thermohaline fields of the Alaskan Beaufort Sea. This was accomplished from five current meter moorings deployed from July 1998 – October 1999 along the shelfbreak and slope of the western, central, and eastern Alaskan Beaufort Sea. The mooring data was supplemented by a novel hydrographic data set obtained from the USN submarine *Hawkbill* in April 1999. The major findings are:

1. The mean monthly along-slope component of the winds was eastward in all months except January 1999, when winds were weakly westward. The monthly wind variance shows no seasonal variation in contrast to climatology, which indicates a doubling in variance from summer to winter.

2. The mean subsurface flow at depths between 80 and 200 meters is eastward along the western and central Beaufort slope. This flow is subject to frequent reversals, which are accompanied by upwelling, but there is no distinct seasonal signal in the shelfbreak flow. This finding contrasts with the large seasonal signal in transport in Bering Strait and over the Chukchi shelf

3. The spatial coherence of the flow field suggests an along-slope decorrelation scale of at least 200 km between the western and central Beaufort shelfbreak. However, along-slope current variations were virtually incoherent between the central and eastern Beaufort Sea. The cross-slope correlation structure suggests that the slope flow field has a complicated structure, which was not adequately resolved with the sampling design and equipment failures.

4. The coherence between winds and along-slope currents varies as a function of depth and distance seaward of the shelfbreak. The largest correlations occur for upper level currents ($\leq \sim 100$ m depth) in the western and central Beaufort Sea. Deeper currents and currents in the eastern Beaufort showed little or no coherence with the winds. The low coherence might be explicable in terms of seasonal variation in the sea ice distribution. It appears that during the winter of 1999, the pack ice was immobile for extensive periods of time in the eastern Beaufort Sea. This implies that little of the surface wind stress is transmitted into the water column, hence the wind-current correlation might be weak due to seasonal and shorter period variations in the ice-water stress. However, in conjunction with conclusion 3, the results suggest that the slope flow is largely influenced by the deep ocean and/or by remotely forced topographic waves.

5. Our results, along with measurements made along the Mackenzie Beaufort slope, suggest that the eastward-flowing Beaufort undercurrent might not extend beyond the eastern portion of the Alaskan Beaufort slope. Instead, the current measurements and hydrography indicate that the eastern Alaskan Beaufort slope might be one of along-slope convergence, wherein the eastward flow in the undercurrent meets the westward flow along the Mackenzie shelfbreak. The merged flows are likely diverted offshore in the form of eddies.

6. We emphasize that the eastern Beaufort mooring may not be representative of conditions at the shelfbreak because the continental slope broadens from west to east. Consequently, this mooring was further seaward of the shelfbreak than the moorings to the west. Very likely we have missed important shelfbreak processes in this region and this caveat must be borne in mind when considering the above conclusions.

7. It seems probable that there is a substantial along-slope density gradient in the vicinity of the Canada/U.S. EEZ line and that this contrast extends across the shelf and has important implications for cross- and along-shelf flows.

I. Introduction

This study examines the subsurface flow along the Alaskan Beaufort continental slope using moored current meters deployed between fall 1998 and 1999 and wintertime hydrography collected by the USN submarine *Hawkbill* in April 1999. The slope is the seaward boundary for the 80 km wide Alaskan Beaufort Sea shelf and slope processes that regulate exchanges between the shelf and basin may be dynamically important to both the shelf and deep basin. For example, *Aagaard et al.* [1989] suggest that during strong westward winds, eastward momentum can be upwelled from the slope onto the Beaufort Sea shelf, perhaps as far inshore as (at least) the 50 m isobath. In such cases, the normally wind-forced westward outer shelf flow reverses and/or slows.

In addition, much of the thermohaline and biogeochemical structure of the Arctic Ocean's interior bears the signature of waters from its adjoining continental shelf seas and from the Pacific and Atlantic oceans [*Aagaard et al.*, 1981; *Jones and Anderson*, 1986]. Central basin waters are therefore largely a result of lateral water mass advection across the shelf/slope margin and through Bering and Fram straits [*Coachman and Barnes*, 1962; *Rudels et al.*, 1994]. Over the Chukchi shelf, the mean flow is northward and carries Pacific waters into the Arctic Ocean. Dynamic principles suggest that much of the Chukchi outflow is first deflected eastward along the continental slope and shelfbreak before entering the central basin. The mechanisms and locations by which this water enters the basin are not well understood, however.

The circulation in the interior ocean (far from the continental shelves and slopes) is weak on average and highly variable in space and time. Instead, the principal advective signatures consist of boundary currents that flow in the direction of Kelvin wave propagation (the bottom shoals to the right of the direction of flow in the northern hemisphere) along the continental slopes and mid-ocean ridges [*Aagaard*, 1989; *Rudels et al.*, 1994]. The boundary currents are subsurface flows and

move in a direction opposite to the wind-driven surface circulation (which extends to ~50 m depth). For this reason *Aagaard* [1984] called the sub-surface currents undercurrents. Hydrographic measurements suggest that the boundary current along the Alaskan Beaufort slope is 10 – 20 km wide [*Pickart*, 2004] and extends over several hundred meters depth. Along the Eurasian continental slope these currents transport Atlantic Water (AW) that enters the eastern Arctic Ocean through Fram Strait and across the Barents Sea shelf [*Steele et al.*, 1995; *McLaughlin et al.*, 2002; *Woodgate et al.*, 2001], mixtures of Barents and Kara shelf waters with Atlantic Water [*Schauer et al.*, 1997] and shelf waters (if sufficiently dense) derived from the Laptev and East Siberian seas. (The shelf water contributions are complex products resulting from river discharge, freezing and melting, and shelfbreak upwelling [*Melling and Moore*, 1995; *Melling*, 1993]. All of these processes affect the density of the shelf water and therefore the depth to which shelf water sinks as it flows across the shelfbreak.) Along the Chukchi and Beaufort shelfbreak, the boundary current incorporates Pacific Ocean waters modified in transit across the Bering and Chukchi shelves [*Aagaard*, 1984; *Carmack*, 1986; *Weingartner et al.*, 1998; *Pickart*, 2004; *Pickart et al.*, accepted; *Weingartner et al.*, accepted; *Woodgate et al.*, accepted]. Thus, the boundary current transports water masses from a variety of sources with each water mass having its own distinct water property signature (which is often distinguishable on the basis of temperature-salinity characteristics or chemical tracers, such as nutrient concentrations or ratios, other naturally occurring dissolved substances, or contaminants). The various water masses contributing to the boundary flows are of different densities, which leads to along-slope variations in density structure. For example, the Pacific outflow from the Chukchi shelf is, on average, less dense than the Atlantic Water modified on the Barents and Kara shelves, which, in turn, is less dense than Atlantic Water flowing through Fram Strait [*McLaughlin et al.*, 2002]. Consequently, there is a progressive thickening of the stratification of the Arctic Ocean as one proceeds eastward from Fram Strait to the Beaufort Sea [*Carmack*, 1986]. Although the stratification varies seasonally (as discussed below), the most prominent (and perennial feature) aspect of the Arctic Ocean's stratification is the halocline between 75 and 200 m depth [**Figure 1**]. Stratification and stratification gradients can affect boundary current dynamics and the exchange of water and momentum between the shelf and slope [*Huthnance*, 1995]. The Alaskan Beaufort continental slope extends 600 km eastward from the Chukchi Sea to the Mackenzie continental shelf in the Canadian Exclusive Economic Zone (**Figure 2**). The bottom slope and width of the continental slope (as determined by the distance between the 100 and 1000 m isobaths) varies from ~0.05 and 20 km in the west to ~0.02 and ~50 km in the east and near the Mackenzie shelf. Seaward of the 3000 m isobath, depths more gradually decrease to more than 4000 m.

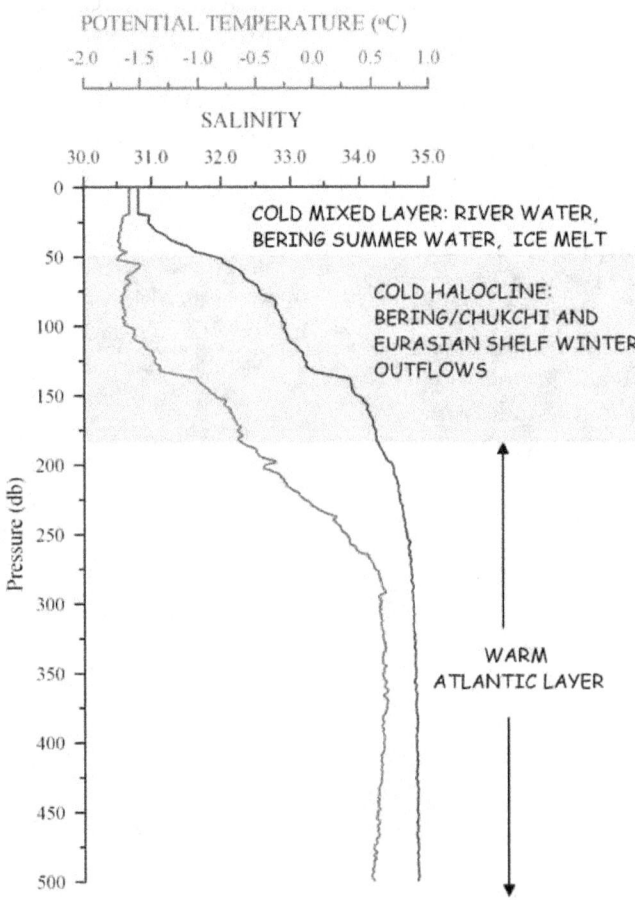

Figure 1: A representative vertical profile of temperature (red) and salinity (blue) obtained along the Beaufort Sea continental slope in April 1999 from XCTDs deployed from the USN *Hawkbill*. The halocline represents the region between 50 and 200 m depth over which the salinity, and hence density, increases rapidly.

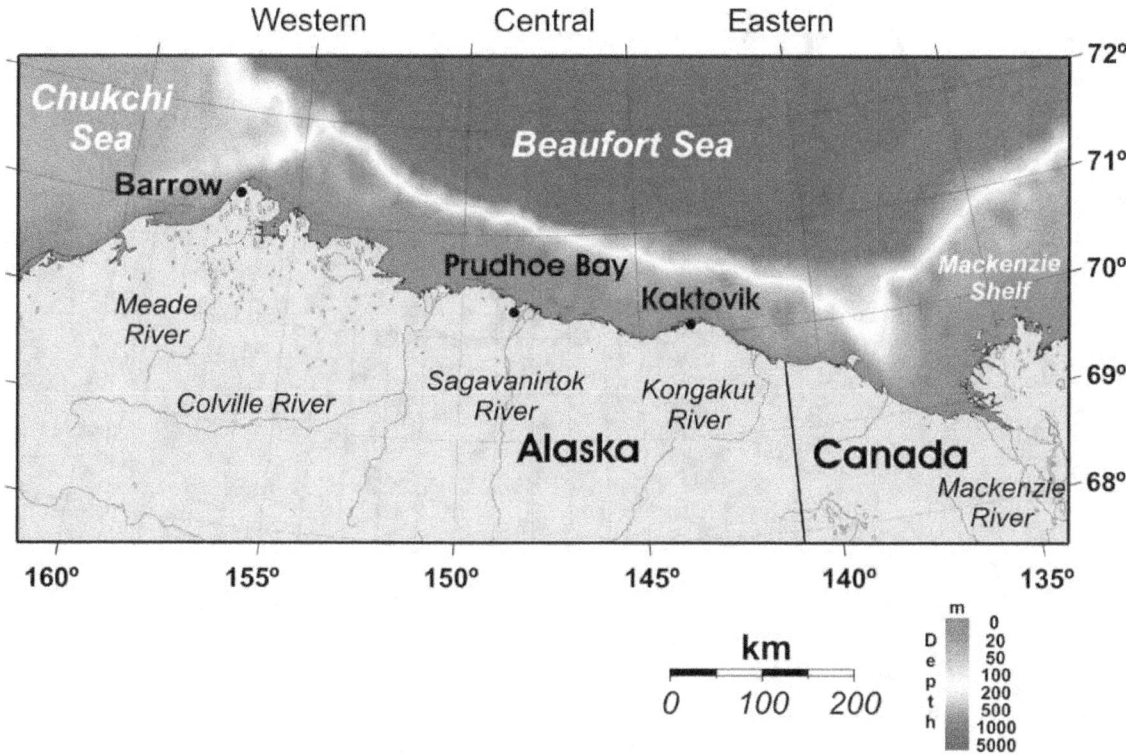

Figure 2: Map of the Alaskan Beaufort Sea and North Slope with place names and subdivisions.

Figure 3 is a schematic of the regional circulation based upon many of the references cited above. The near-surface (0 – 50 m depth, at least) circulation over the continental slope is westward and consists of the southern limb of the wind-forced Beaufort Gyre. Between 50 and 175 m, the flow is eastward and transports waters derived from the Chukchi Sea shelf. (Hereafter, we follow *Aagaard's* [1984] terminology and refer to this eastward subsurface flow as the undercurrent.) These waters originate in the Pacific Ocean (Bering Sea) and flow northward through Bering Strait at a long-term mean rate of 0.8 Sv [Sverdrups; 1 Sv = 10^6 m^3 s^{-1}; *Roach et al.* 1995]. North of the strait, the Pacific waters flow across the Chukchi shelf along three principal pathways associated with major topographic depressions in the western, eastern, and central Chukchi Sea [*Weingartner et al.,* accepted; *Woodgate et al.,* accepted]. The density of these outflows varies seasonally, but the denser fractions, formed in winter through cooling and brine enhancement during ice formation, feed the shallower portion of the undercurrent and upper halocline.

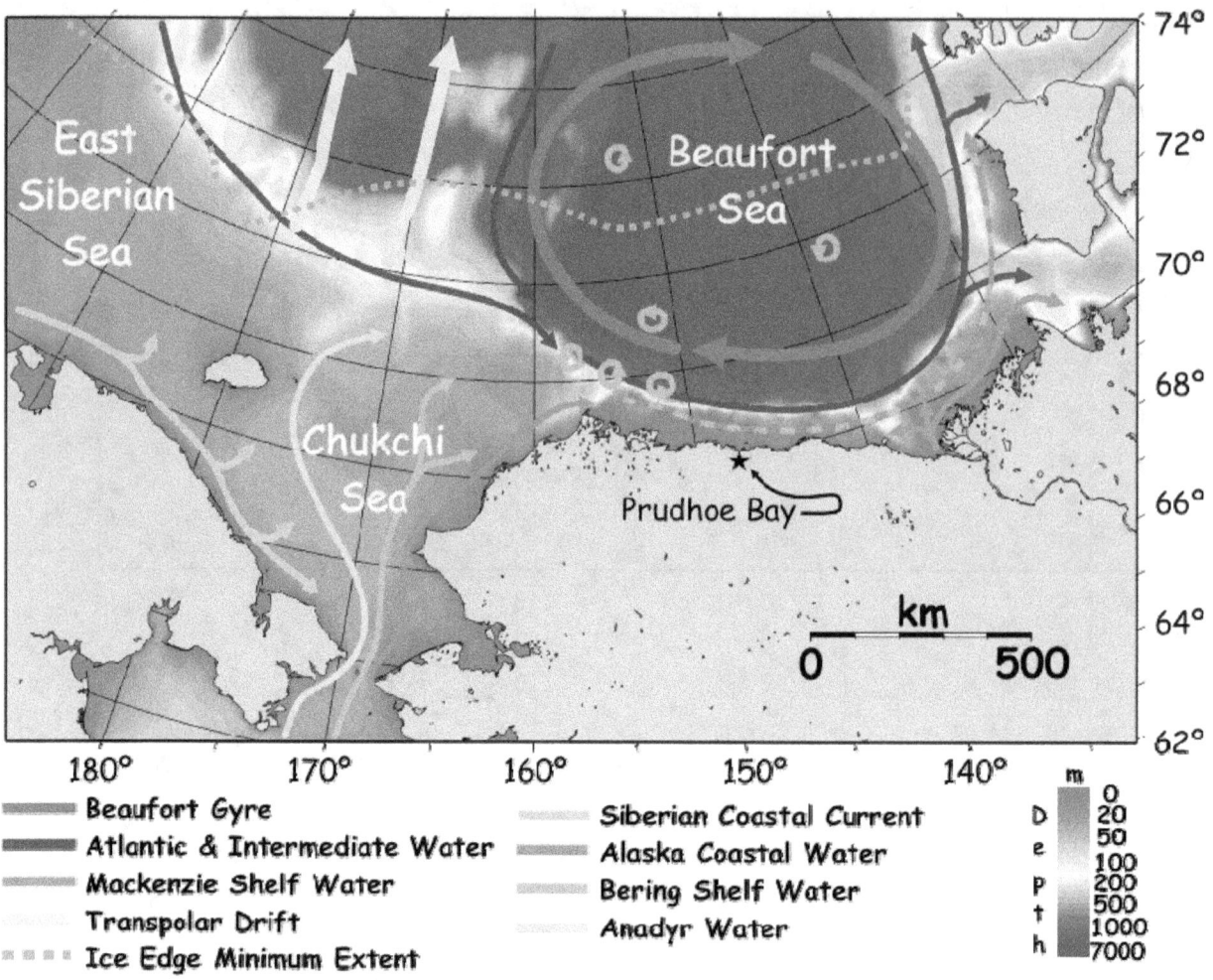

Figure 3: Regional circulation schematic of the Beaufort Sea illustrating connections to adjacent shelves and the Canada Basin.

Of particular relevance to the present study is that the easternmost branch of the Chukchi Sea outflow joins the Beaufort slope at the mouth of Barrow Canyon, although some of this outflow might spill onto the Beaufort Sea shelf as well [*Aagaard*, 1984; *Pickart et al.*, accepted]. Waters from the western and central Chukchi outflows also appear to flow eastward along the slope to eventually join with the outflow from Barrow Canyon. Not all of the water exiting the Chukchi shelf enters the boundary current, however, for *Shimada et al.* [2001] show that the less dense waters leaving the Chukchi shelf in summer enter the near-surface layers of the Beaufort Gyre and are carried westward and thence northwestward into the Canada Basin. In addition, the slope current is inherently unstable [*Pickart*, 2004] and therefore capable of generating the numerous mesoscale eddies (20 km diameter and ~100 m vertical extent) that populate the interior of the Canada Basin [*Newton* et al., 1974, *Manley and Hunkins*, 1985; *Muench et al.*, 2000]. Recent NSF-sponsored research conducted by Aagaard, Pickart, Weingartner, and Woodgate along the northern Chukchi slope suggests that the eddies (depicted as small clockwise rotating circles in **Figure 3**) are common features of the slope between at least the central Chukchi and western Beaufort slope. Whether or not eddy formation occurs along the central and eastern portions of the Alaskan Beaufort Sea remains unknown.

Beneath the halocline (**Figure 1**), salinities slowly increase with depth, but temperatures increase to a subsurface maximum of ~0.7°C at 300 m, and then decrease more slowly to 0.0°C at about 800 m depth. This warm layer originates in the Atlantic Ocean and flows around the continental slopes and along the major topographic ridges of the Arctic Ocean. It is modified en route through cooling with overlying ice (in the Nansen Basin) and through contributions from the Eurasian shelf seas [*McLaughlin et al.*, 2002]. Most likely the majority of the Atlantic-influenced waters flow southward along the Northwind Ridge north of the Chukchi Sea and then turn eastward along the Beaufort slope (**Figure 3**). There may also be an additional eastward flow of Atlantic-modified water along the Chukchi continental slope. The thermohaline characteristics of Atlantic waters do not vary seasonally, although there have been substantial changes in the temperature of these waters in the last decade [*McLaughlin et al.*, 2002, 2004].

The eastern sector of the Alaskan Beaufort continental slope connects to the Mackenzie shelf/slope in the vicinity of Mackenzie Canyon near 140°W (**Figure 2**). Here the along-slope isobaths diverge so that the continental slope broadens and becomes not as steep. Moreover, we expect that the thermohaline properties over the slope will also change in this region due to the outflow of water from the Mackenzie shelf. Mackenzie shelf water is substantially influenced by the year-round discharge from the Mackenzie River [*Carmack et al.*, 1989; *Macdonald et al.*, 1989; *Macdonald and Carmack*, 1991] although its density varies seasonally and interannually depending upon the winds and the amount of ice produced on the Mackenzie shelf [*Melling*, 1993]. In summer, brackish Mackenzie water can spread far across the shelf and into the Canada Basin as a shallow surface layer (~25 – 50 m thick). The horizontal extent of this dispersal probably varies from year to year depending upon the strength, frequency, and duration of northeasterly (upwelling-favorable) winds (which prevail on average) over this shelf. Mackenzie shelf waters have been detected along the continental slope of the Chukchi and western Beaufort Sea as far west as 160°W [*Guay and Falkner*, 1997; *MacDonald et al.*, 1999a]. In years of frequent or strong downwelling winds, however, much of the Mackenzie River's summer discharge is probably advected northeastward along Banks Island or into the Canadian Archipelago [*Melling*, 1993]. In winter, the Mackenzie shelf can be a source of moderately saline shelf water formed through enhanced ice production (and brine expulsion) in the flaw lead that develops offshore of the landfast ice edge [*Macdonald and Carmack*, 1991]. This dense water can ventilate the upper halocline [*Melling*, 1993; and *Melling and Moore*, 1995] and, by so doing, alter the along-slope density gradient.

The slope flow is expected to vary seasonally given the substantial annual variation in the regional winds, the Chukchi shelf transport that feeds the undercurrent, and the density of the outflowing shelf waters from both

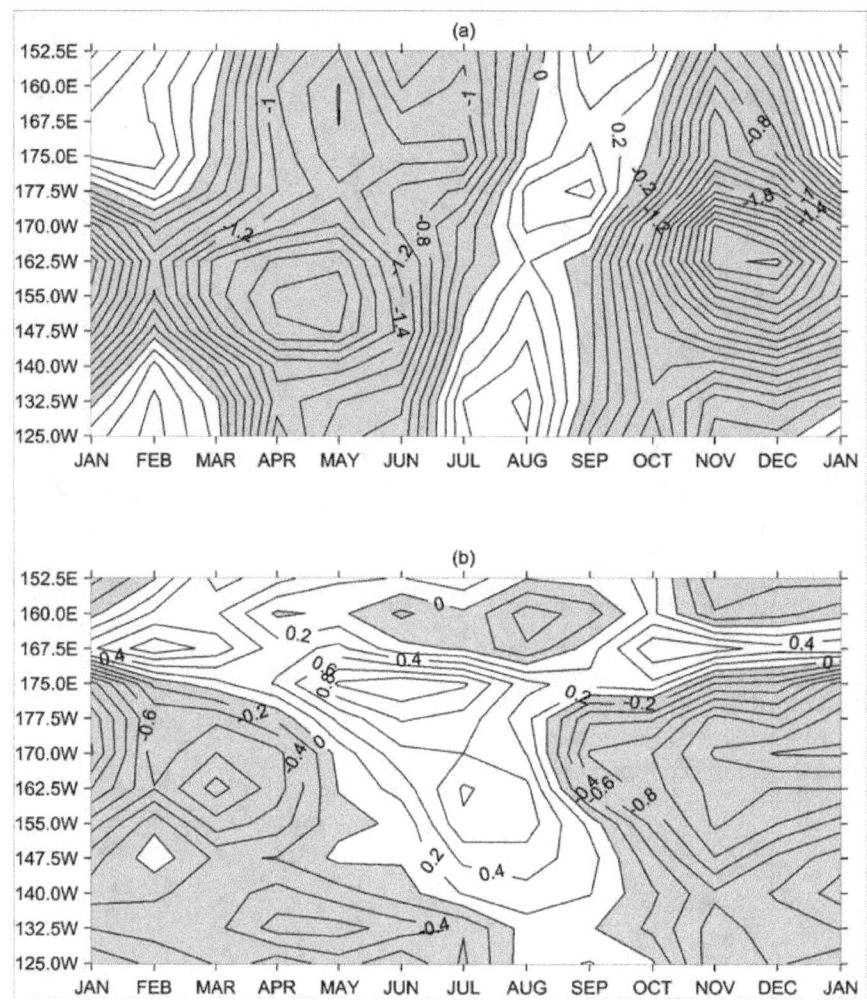

Figure 4: Time-longitude plots of mean monthly a) east-west (~along-slope) and b) north-south (~cross-slope) wind component along 72.5°N. Contour interval is 0.2 m s⁻¹ [*Furey*, 1998]. Positive values indicate winds blowing to the east or north and negative values indicate winds blowing to the west or south.

the Chukchi and Mackenzie shelves. *Furey's* [1996] analysis of the 1981–1993 surface winds (derived from the U.S. Navy's forecast wind fields) shows a distinct annual cycle in the along-slope winds in both the east-west and north-south components (**Figure 4**) for the region between 152.5°E (East Siberian Sea) to 125°W (Mackenzie shelf). The winds are primarily zonal year-round and over the Alaskan Beaufort Sea they are westward in all seasons except in summer when they are weakly eastward. Maximum wind speeds occur in fall (Nov.–Dec.) and early spring (Apr.–May) and

are centered over the western Beaufort slope. The north-south wind component is weak throughout the year and is weakly southward from fall through spring and weakly northward in summer. While the winds vary over a range of time scales shorter than the seasonal, the along-slope coherence scale of these variations is generally ~1000 km [*Furey*, 1998].

The western Beaufort slope incorporates the outflow from Barrow Canyon, with that transport varying both seasonally and synoptically [**Figure 5**; *Weingartner et al.*, in prep.] in response to the along-slope winds

[*Weingartner et al.*, 1998; accepted]. The long-term mean transport through the canyon is about 0.3 Sv (into the Arctic Ocean). It has a maximum of ~0.6 Sv in August and a minimum (0 Sv) in December. The average transport in the canyon is less than half the mean transport through Bering Strait, but it varies seasonally and in-phase with the Bering Strait transport [**Figure 5**; bottom panel]. Mean daily canyon transports can vary rapidly and range from -2 Sv (negative values indicate upcanyon transport or transport onto the Chukchi shelf) to 1.5 Sv downcanyon.

The density of the Chukchi shelf outflow varies seasonally with the saltiest (densest)

fraction exiting the shelf from winter through late summer and the freshest flowing offshelf in late summer and fall [*Weingartner et al.*, 1998; accepted; *Woodgate et al.*, accepted]. The different densities ventilate the continental slope at different depths with the fresher components mixing with the surface waters over the slope while the most saline fraction can ventilate the halocline between 100 and 175 m [*Weingartner*, accepted; *Woodgate et al.*, accepted]. In summary the transport, temperature, and salinity of Chukchi shelf waters (nearly all of which are derived from Pacific Ocean waters flowing through Bering Strait) vary seasonally and affect

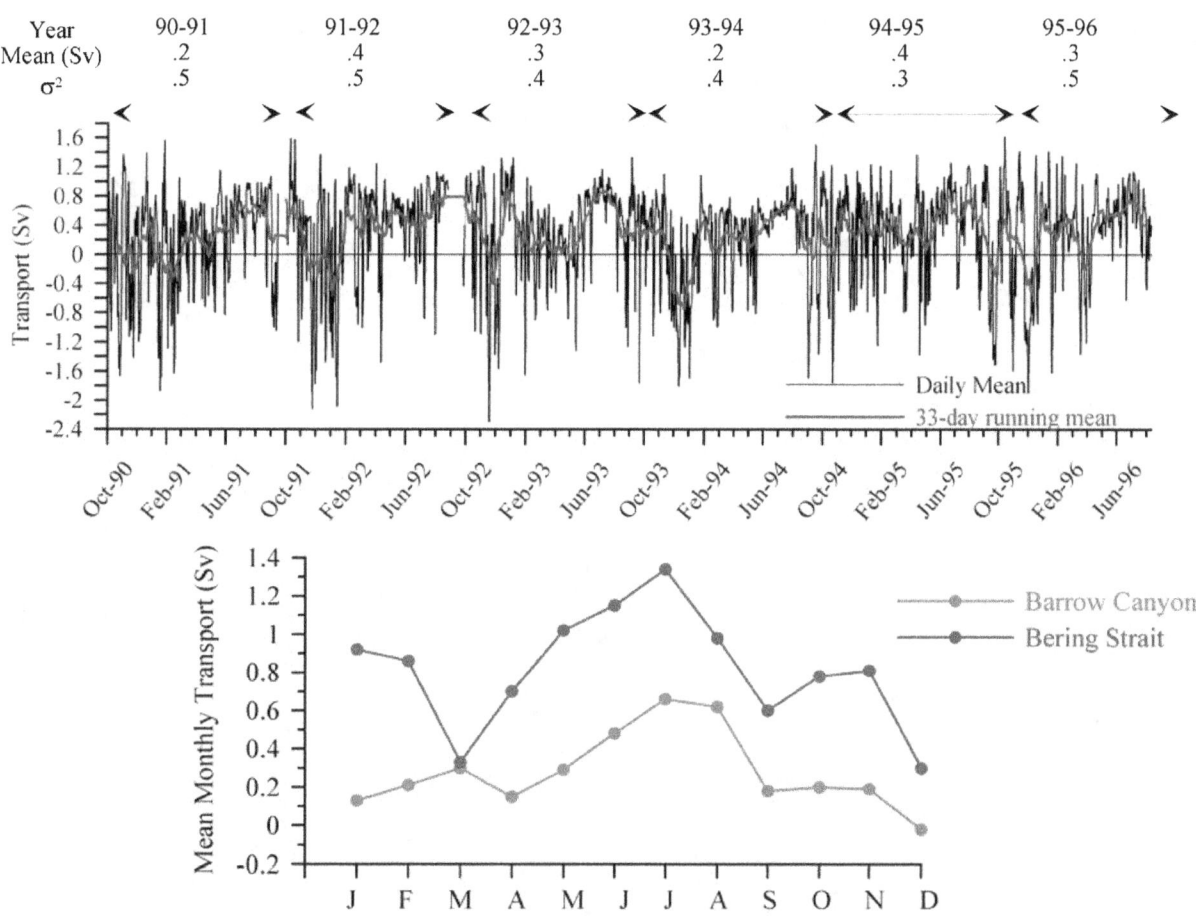

Figure 5: Upper panel: Mean daily transport through Barrow Canyon (black lines) and 33-day running mean of the daily transports (blue line). Lower panel: Mean monthly transports in Bering Strait (blue; from *Roach et al.*, 1995) and from Barrow Canyon (red; from *Weingartner et al.*, in prep.).

conditions along the Alaskan Beaufort slope and shelfbreak.

The differences in the vertical profiles of temperature and salinity for winter and summer are shown in **Figure 6**, (both profiles collected along the continental slope of the western Beaufort Sea in April [winter] and September [summer]). The largest seasonal differences are in the upper 150 m. In summer, the temperature profile shows a complex structure associated with interleaving lenses of relatively warm

water, from $1 - 3°C$, with cold ($\sim-1.0°C$). Much of the warm water is the inflow of Bering Summer Water from the Chukchi shelf (perhaps mixed with dilute but warm ice melt waters). Salinities range from $29 - 31$ in the upper 100 m and are fresh relative to winter due to terrestrial runoff and ice-melt. Winter temperatures in the upper 100 m are within a few tenths of a degree of the freezing point. Salinities in the upper 50 m are vertically uniform at ~31 and rapidly

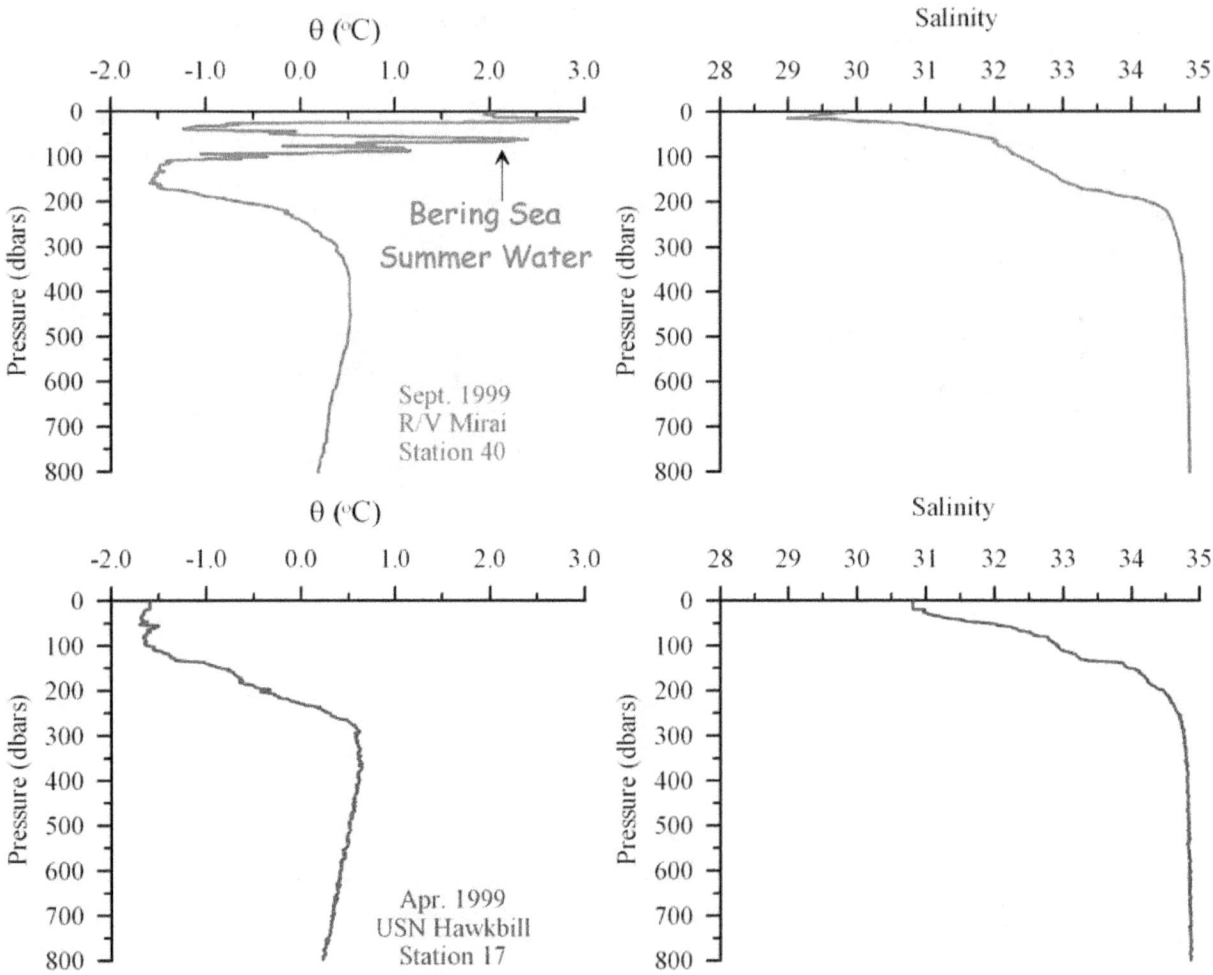

Figure 6: Vertical profiles (0 – 800 db) of temperature and salinity along the western Beaufort Sea continental slope from summer (red) and winter (blue). Summer data provide by K. Shimada (JAMSTEC).

8

increase with depth to about 34.5 at 200 m. The lower halocline, as defined by salinities between 33 – 34, is approximately 35 m shallower in winter than in summer.

To date there has been no systematic investigation of undercurrent dynamics in the Arctic Ocean, although several hypotheses have been advanced to explain its existence. For example, Holloway [1992] and Haidvogel and Brink [1986] show that eddy-topographic interactions can generate rectified (mean) currents that flow in the direction of Kelvin wave propagation. Of particular relevance to the Alaskan Beaufort setting is Gawarkiewicz's [2000] finding that the undercurrent might arise through rectification of an eddy flow field generated when dense shelf water flows across the shelfbreak. As noted above, dense outflows of halocline source waters occur nearly year-round from the Chukchi shelf. The undercurrents might also arise as a geostrophic adjustment of the inflows from the adjacent shelves and/or oceans as found for undercurrents elsewhere in the global ocean [Ponte, 1995; Kundu and McCreary, 1986]. Other dynamics might also be involved, however. For example, the Beaufort undercurrent could be dynamically analogous to the poleward flowing countercurrents found along the eastern boundaries of mid-latitude oceans [McCreary, 1981; Philander and Yoon, 1982] or due to the existence of an along-slope density (or baroclinic pressure) gradient over a continental slope, e.g., the "JEBAR" (Joint Effect of Baroclinicity and Relief) mechanism [Huthnance, 1984, 1995] or "pycnobathic" currents [Csanady, 1985]. While it is probably that more than one process is operating along the Chukchi-Beaufort slope, we show below that there is a substantial along-shelf density gradient that suggests that JEBAR dynamics could be an important component in the dynamics of the flow field along the Alaskan Beaufort slope. Our results also raise important questions regarding the continuity of the undercurrent along the eastern Beaufort slope.

II. Objectives

The purpose of this program was to provide a kinematical and, where possible, dynamical description of the circulation, thermohaline structure, and cross-slope transport along the Beaufort Sea shelfbreak and slope. The field and data analysis portions of the program were designed to address the following issues:

1. Determine the mean transport over the outer shelf and slope and the cross-slope and vertical scales of the mean flow field.

2. Determine the magnitudes of transport variability and the dominant temporal and spatial scales associated with this variability.

3. Determine the cross-slope fluxes of heat, salt, and momentum. Determine if these are related to instabilities (eddy generation mechanisms) of the along-slope flow.

4. Determine the relationship between observed flow and density variations and the surface wind field.

5. Compare the results obtained from the proposed field program with those collected in 1987/88 by Aagaard et al., [1989], to determine if the present set of measurements are comparable to those obtained earlier.

We were only modestly successful in achieving these goals due, in part, to equipment failure and loss. In particular neither estimates of along-slope transport nor cross-slope fluxes could be reliably made.

III. Methods

The field program consisted of two distinct elements: an array of six moorings sponsored by MMS (and conducted in collaboration with the Japan Marine Science and Technology Center; JAMSTEC) and a winter hydrography program led by Weingartner and supported by the Office of Naval Research. **Figure 7** shows the locations of the moorings and the hydrographic stations occupied during April 1999 by the U.S. Navy submarine *Hawkbill*. Six moorings (two, BF-K-98 and BF-S-98, were sponsored and prepared by JAMSTEC, a matching partner in this program) were deployed in September 1998 from the *Sir Wilfred Laurier*, a Canadian Coast Guard icebreaker. (Ship logistics constituted

additional matched support from the Canadian Coast Guard.) The original plan called for 1 mooring (BF-K-98) to be deployed in the western Beaufort Sea and for five moorings (B1, BF-S-98, B3, B4 and B5) to be deployed across the central Beaufort Sea slope. After the first four moorings were deployed along the central slope, several days of severe weather prevented additional work. Although the vessel stood by for 2 days awaiting the weather to abate, it did not, and scheduling requirements necessitated that it continue eastward. We therefore elected to deploy mooring B5 along about the 1000 m isobath over the

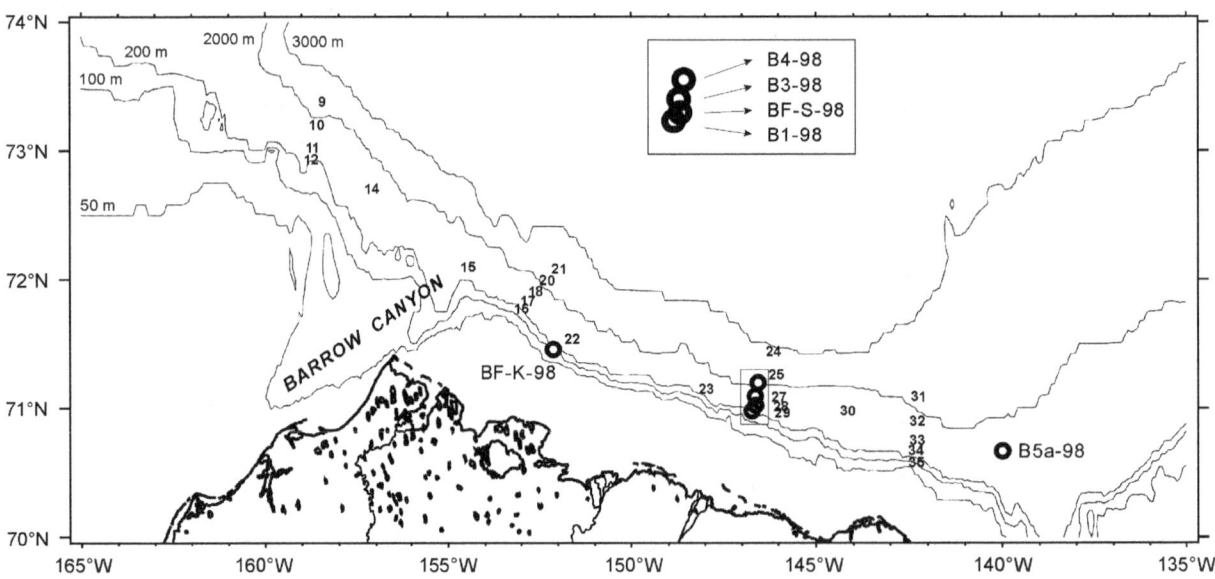

Figure 7: Map showing the location of the moorings (open circles) and hydrographic stations (centered on the numbers). Stations 13 and 19 had faulty XCTDs and are not shown. The dotted line shows the approximate location of the submarine's along-slope transect from which temperature and salinity data were collected continuously while underway.

eastern Beaufort slope. All moorings, except B4 were recovered in October 1999 by the *Sir Wilfred Laurier*. B4 did not respond to acoustic release commands and poor weather and the ship schedule constraints required that we abandon mooring search and recovery operations. In fall 2000, the *Sir Wilfred Laurier* once again transited eastward along the Alaskan Beaufort Sea and spent an additional day conducting an unsuccessful search for mooring B4. The mooring was likely dragged from its position by drifting sea ice and either destroyed or moved far outside the search grid. It is also possible that the batteries failed in the acoustic releases (although these had sufficient power for a three-year deployment). All the moorings were taut-line, subsurface moorings having a variety of instruments, including temperature-conductivity recorders (Seabird SeaCats or MicroCats), acoustic Doppler current profilers (ADCP), electromagnetic (Aanderaa RCM8 or S4), or Aanderaa current meters equipped with rotors (RCM 4, 5, or 7). The mooring positions, deployment depths and the institution responsible for the mooring (JAMSTEC, UAF, or UW) are listed in **Table 1**. Instrument types, record lengths, and data quality comments for each instrument are listed in **Tables 2 – 4**. Numerous instrument problems plagued the data set, especially with the Aanderaa meters equipped with rotors. The two most common problems were rotor stalls and/or premature battery failure. The former were due either to clogging by suspended material or because current speeds were below the rotor threshold speed ($\sim$3 cm s^{-1}). There were also several failures with the temperature/conductivity recorders resulting in either reduced data record length or outright failure of the instrument due to leakage upon deployment.

The number of failures was unusually large based on prior experience and suggests an unlucky combination of events. However, the large number of short Aanderaa record lengths might also be due to a batch of bad batteries (all batteries were new prior to deployment). Many of the Aanderaa RCM 4, 5, and 7s were also old (> 15 years old), which might have contributed to some of the failures in this instrument pool. Finally, we have had only one failure due to flooding of a Seacat T/C recorder in over 10 years of deploying these instruments.

Table 1: 1998 Beaufort Sea Mooring Deployments

Mooring ID	Isobath (m)	Latitude (N)	Longitude (W)	Organization
WESTERN BEAUFORT				
BF-K-98	128	71° 23.0'	152° 04.72'	JAMSTEC
CENTRAL BEAUFORT				
B1-98	86	70° 54.3'	146° 41.15'	UAF
BF-S-98	500	70° 56.94'	146° 35.48'	JAMSTEC
B3-98	1302	71° 00.78'	146° 36.58'	UAF/UW
B4-98*	1700	71° 07.46'	146° 31.27'	UAF/UW
WESTERN BEAUFORT				
B5a-98	990	70° 35.62'	139° 57.54'	UAF/UW

*mooring lost

Winter hydrographic measurements were made with expendable conductivity-temperature-depth (XCTD) probes and continuous underway temperature and salinity

11

(UTS) measurements from a temperature-conductivity recorder mounted in the submarine's sail. The XCTDs are launched through the submarine's torpedo tubes at depth (~110 m). After launch, the probe rises to a depth of about 12 m and then begins its descent to a nominal terminal depth of 750 m or shallower if the bottom is encountered. CTD data are transmitted through a wire connected to the submarine during the descent. At the end of the profile the XCTD wire breaks and the cast is completed. The UTS measurements consist of 6 minute-averaged samples of temperature and salinity at a depth of 117 m (±1 m) collected along about the 500 m isobath while the submarine was in transit.

Pre- and post-calibrations suggest that the salinity measurements are better than 0.03 for salinity (using the non-dimensional Practical Salinity Scale) and better than 0.01°C for temperature for the Aanderaa instruments and better than 0.01 for salinity and <0.01°C for temperature from the SeaCats or MicroCats, including the SeaCat mounted on the submarine's sail.

Table 2: Record lengths for the western Beaufort mooring array. Current meters and T/C recorders.

Mooring	Depth	Start_date (YMDhms	End_date (YMDhms	Records (#)	Comments
BFK_R1[1] (RCM7)	72	98/07/21 1800	99/10/1 0700	10478	Good
BFK_R2[1,2] (RCM8)	104	98/07/21 1800	99/08/19 1300	9452	Battery failed 8/19
BFK_R3[1,2] (RCM9)	116	98/07/21 1800	99/07/21 1800	9021	Battery failed 7/21
BFK_R4[1,2] (RCM9)	123	98/07/21 1800	99/07/21 1800	9021	Battery failed 7/21
BFK_ADCP (600kHz)	82 – 122	98/07/21 1800	99/10/10 1600	10703	Good

[1]Aanderaa RCM (7, 8 and/or 9) with temperature and conductivity
[2]Velocity record not used because of shortened length and/or redundant with ADCP depths

Table 3: Record lengths for the central Beaufort mooring array. Current meters (R) and T/C recorders (S).

Mooring	Depth	Start_date (YMDhms	End_date (YMDhms	Records (#)	Comments
B1_R1*(RCM7)	52	98/07/25 2300	98/11/15 0900	2699	Battery failed 11/16/98 *Not used*
B1_R2*(RCM7)	72	98/07/26 0000	99/09/20 1800	10123	Rotor sticking in March and April
BFS_R1 (RCM8)	101	98/07/25 1900	99/07/15 0000	8502	Good
BFS_R2 (RCM8)	192	98/07/25 1900	99/06/02 0000	7476	Good through 3/99 – rotor stalls afterwards
BFS_R3 (RCM8)	251	98/07/25 1900	99/02/11 0900	4839	Bad speed *Not used*
BFS_R4 (S4)	413	98/07/25 1900	99/10/09 1700	10583	Good
BFS_S1 (SC)	73	98/07/25 1900	99/10/09 1700	10583	Good
BFS_S2 (SC)	133	98/07/25 1900	99/10/09 1700	10583	Good
BFS_S3 (MC)	163	98/07/25 1900	99/09/06 0000	900	Flooded *Not used*
BFS_S4 (MC)	193	98/07/25 1900	99/10/09 1700	10583	Good
BFS_S4 (MC)	223	98/07/29 2300	99/10/09 1700	10583	Good
BFS_S5 (MC)	253	98/07/25 1900	99/10/09 1700	10583	Good
B3_R1(RCM7)	254	98/07/25 1200	99/09/21 1400	10155	Good
B3_R2(RCM7)	355	98/07/25 1100	99/09/21 1400	10156	Rotor stalled after 4/99 truncated at 4/30/99
B3_R3(RCM7)	503	98/07/25 1200	99/08/26 1000	9527	Rotor stalls after 4/99- truncated at 4/30/99
B3_R4(RCM4)	1002	98/07/25 1300	98/12/23 2300	3635	Battery failed/rotor stalls throughout record *Not used*

*Aanderaa RCM7 with temperature and conductivity

Table 4: Record lengths for the eastern Beaufort mooring array. Current meters (R) and T/C recorders (S).

Mooring	Depth	Start_date (YMDhms	End_date (YMDhms	# of samples	Comments
B5_R1(RCM7)	28	98/07/28 0000	99/06/07 0700	7544	Good
B5_R2(RCM7)	128	98/07/27 2300	99/09/27 1900	10245	Good
B5_R3(RCM7)	227	98/07/28 0300	99/10/03 2000	10386	Good
B5_R4(RCM7)	476	98/07/28 0800	99/10/03 2000	10381	Good
B5_S1 (SC)	38	98/07/28 0000	99/10/03 2200	10389	Good
B5_S2 (MC)	103	98/07/28 0000	99/10/03 2200	10389	Good
B5_S3 (SC)	177	98/07/28 0000	99/10/03 2200	10389	Good
B5_S4 (MC)	276	98/07/28 0000	99/10/03 2200	10389	Good

For the western Beaufort mooring (BFK), we use the ADCP record for velocities, since these are similar to the Aanderaa current meters, but yielded longer record lengths. However, we use the temperature and salinity data recorded by the Aanderaas at this mooring.

IV. Results

IV.1 Winds

The mean monthly east-west (~along-slope) and north-south (~cross-slope) winds over the Beaufort Sea slope using the observed winds at Barrow and the European Center for Medium-Range Weather Forecasting (ECMWF) winds from July 1998 – October 1999 are shown for comparison in **Figures 8 and 9**. The monthly statistics (means and standard deviations) for the two sites are similar, although the ECMWF cross-slope wind speeds are generally greater than the observed winds at Barrow. Those differences may be real or an artifact of the boundary layer correction applied to the ECMWF geostrophic winds. In agreement with climatology, the mean monthly winds were primarily westward and maximum wind speeds occur in October–November and April–May. However, the mean winds during summer (July and August) were westward, whereas the climatology indicates mean eastward winds during these months. In fact, only in January 1999 were the monthly-averaged winds eastward. Moreover, the observed monthly variances are more or less uniform throughout the year in contrast to the climatology, which indicates that wind variance doubles between summer and winter [*Furey*, 1996].

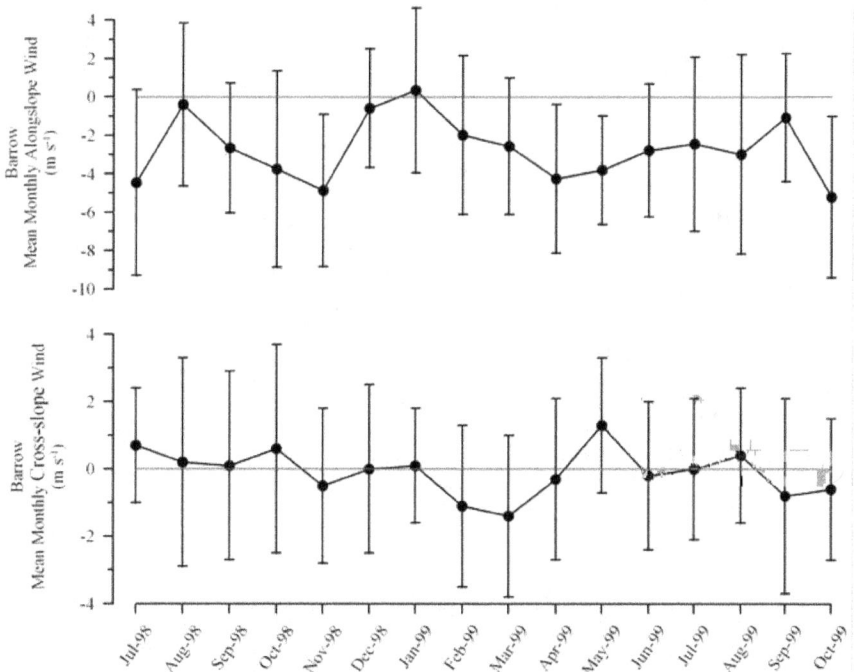

Figure 8: Mean monthly Barrow wind speeds for the along-slope (east-west) and cross-slope (north-south) velocity component. Filled circles are the mean monthly values and bars indicate the monthly standard deviation. Positive values indicate winds blowing to the east or north and negative values indicate winds blowing to the west or south.

15

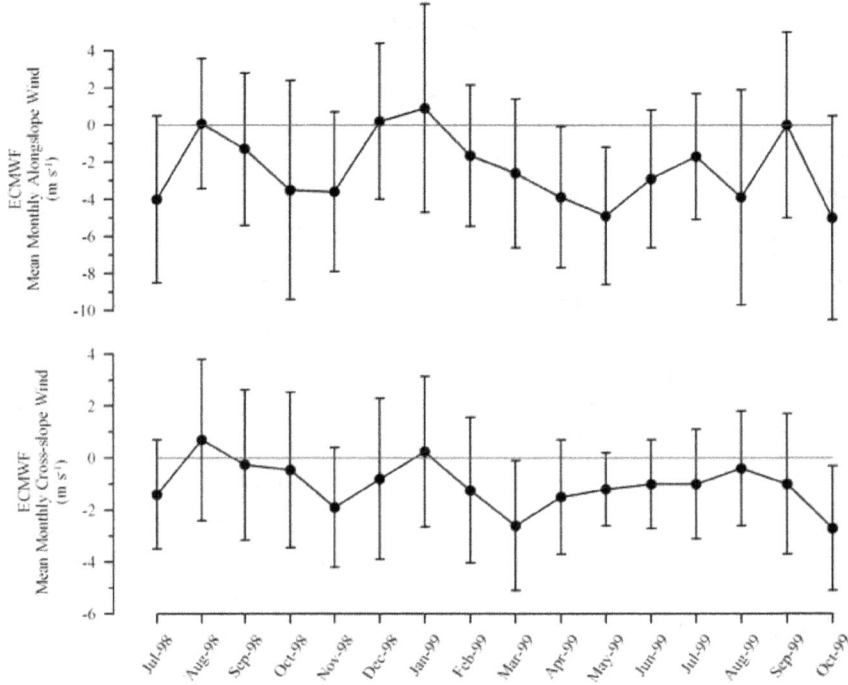

Figure 9: Mean monthly ECMWF (71° 12.8'N, 147° 22.5'W) wind speeds for the along-slope (east-west) and cross-slope (north-south) velocity component. Filled circles are the mean monthly values and bars indicate the monthly standard deviation. Positive values indicate winds blowing to the east or north and negative values indicate winds blowing to the west or south.

The large monthly standard deviations are a consequence of shorter-period wind variations shown for the along-slope wind velocity and wind stress (**Figures 10 and 11,** respectively). Westward winds promote westward surface flow and upwelling and eastward winds force eastward surface flow and downwelling. The strongest westward or upwelling-favorable wind stress occurred from October – November 1998, April – June 1999, and August 1999. Eastward or downwelling favorable wind stress magnitudes are smaller and downwelling events rarely last for more than 10 days, although, as noted above, downwelling favorable winds prevailed in January 1999.

16

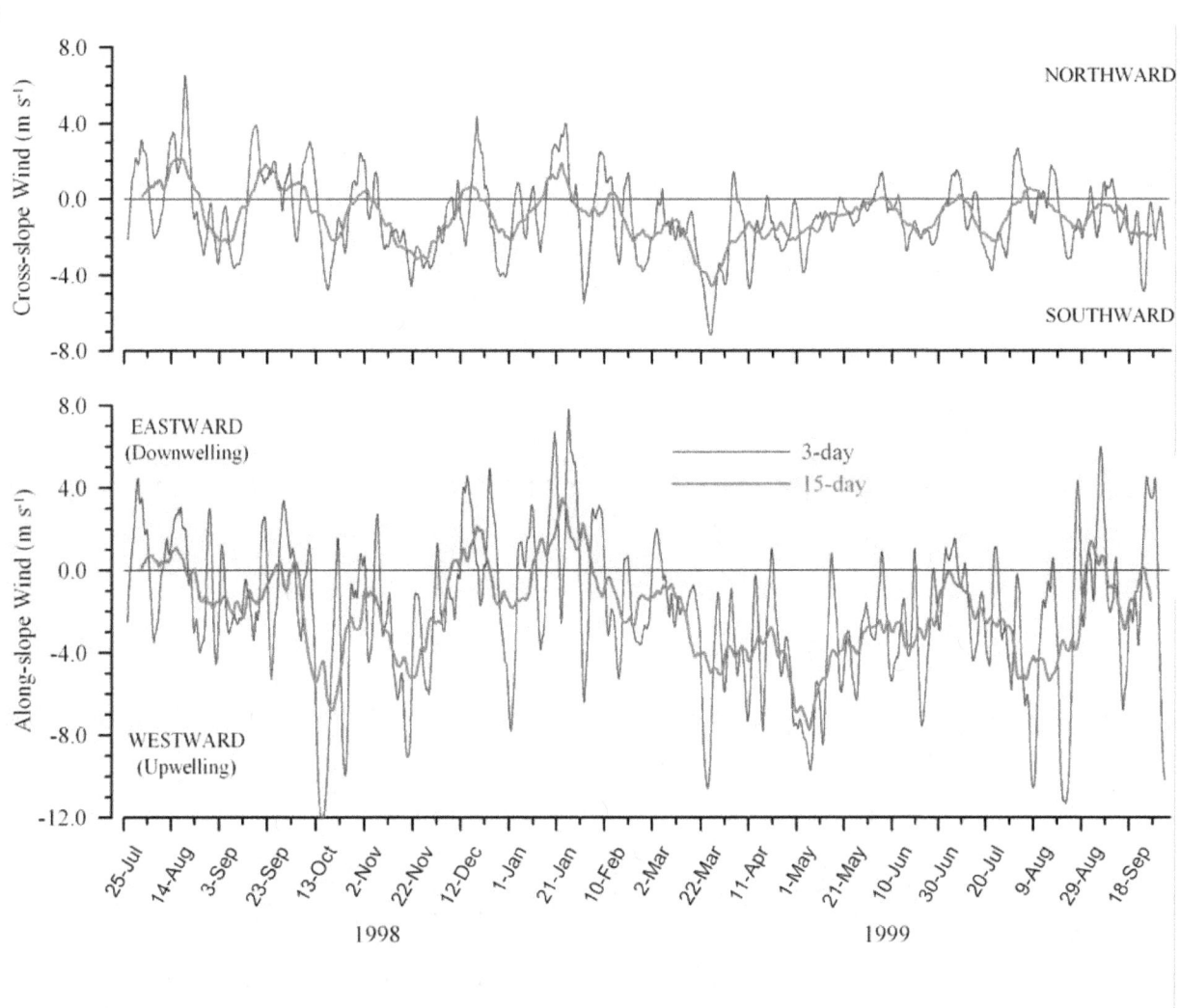

Figure 10: 3-day and 15-day running means of the cross-slope (upper panel) and along-slope (lower panel) ECMWF winds at 71° 12.8'N, 147° 22.5'W.

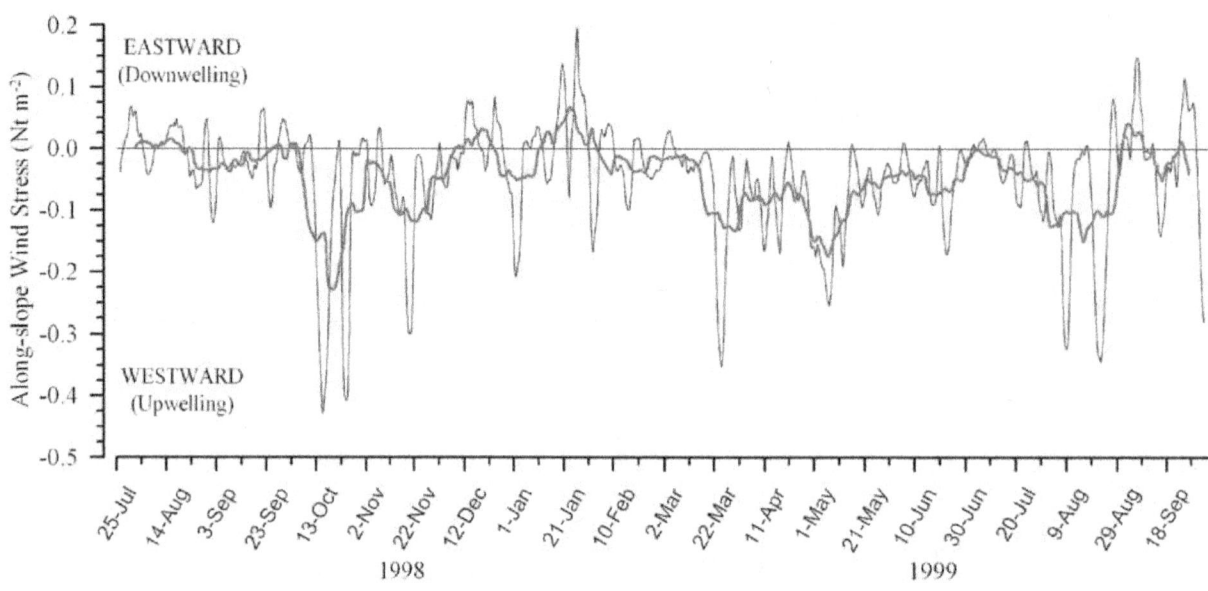

Figure 11: Along-slope wind stress estimated from ECMWF winds at 71° 12.8'N, 147° 22.5' W after smoothing with a 3-day (blue) and 15-day (red) running mean.

IV.2 Currents

Record length current statistics are summarized in **Table 5** (mooring BFK) and **Table 6** (central moorings, B1, BFS, B3 and eastern mooring B5). At the western mooring (BFK) the mean flow components are both statistically significant with the flow toward the east-southeast at a mean speed of ~5 cm s^{-1}. The mean southward velocity of ~1 cm s^{-1} (not statistically significant) is nevertheless consistent with the dynamic topography obtained from the submarine hydrography (shown later), which indicates a mean southward geostrophic flow of the same magnitude over the upper 100 m of the water column. The flow varies primarily in the east-west direction as indicated by the principal axis projection, with > 90% of the flow variance aligned in the along-slope direction and parallel to the isobaths. Mean flows at the central mooring site are also eastward on average, with the majority of the flow variance (> 75%) oriented in the along-slope direction.

For all moorings the principal axis of variance is roughly aligned parallel to the isobaths, with approximately 80% or more of the variance explained by this projection. The integral time scales at moorings BFK, B1, and BFS are all < 6 days, indicating relatively short period current fluctuations. However, at mooring B3, the integral time scales are longer, suggesting that longer period phenomena dominate the motion moving seaward and deeper in the water column.

In summary, both the western and central moorings show a mean eastward flow, albeit with substantial current variability. Both the mean and varying components of the flow parallel the isobaths suggesting that the currents are largely steered by the topography.

In contrast to the western and central moorings, the east-west velocity components at the eastern mooring are not statistically significant, except at 476 m, where an eastward flow of about 1 cm s^{-1} is indicated. The north-south (~cross-slope) flow components are small (~1 cm s^{-1}), although significant, and indicate a mean northward flow at 28 m depth but a mean southward flow at the deeper depths. As with the central mooring there is a dichotomy in the integral time scales between the shallowest meter and the deeper instruments suggesting longer period motions at depth and shorter period motions at the 28 m. At the three shallowest depths only about 65% of the variance is aligned along the principle axis of variance and the orientation of these axes is in the east-northeast sector. Only at 476 m is the axis of principle variance oriented toward the southeast (as are the isobaths) and here ~87% of the variance is accounted for by this projection. These features suggest that the topographic control on the flow at the eastern site is weaker than at the central or western moorings except at 476 m. This is most likely due to the decreasing bathymetric gradient in the continental slope of the eastern Beaufort Sea. The lack of the mean eastward flow at 128 m and 227 m indicates that the undercurrent has disappeared or that is has migrated further inshore and closer to the shelfbreak.

In general, the variance decreases with depth at all moorings, although the maximum variance was observed at ~100 m depth at BFS_R2 along the central array. The reason for this is not known, although the instrument is located near the heart of undercurrent (*Aagaard*, 1984; *Pickart*, 2004).

Low-pass filtered velocity component time series for each good quality current record are shown in **Figures 12 – 20**. (Note that the velocity scales change among plots.) The time series illustrate the rich temporal and spatial structure in the variability of the along- and cross-slope currents. While inspection of the various records suggests some coherency in the current fluctuations, the overall appearance is that correlation structure is complicated and variable both spatially and temporally.

For example, both the along- and cross-slope velocity components at mooring BFK in the western Beaufort Sea are highly coherent, with most of the current variance between 82 – 122 m in-phase and coherent. There is, however, no strong seasonal signal in these data in contrast to the large seasonality identified in the Barrow Canyon transport climatology (**Figure 5**). We explore the wind-current relationships below after first describing in more detail the spatial and temporal structure of the current field.

IV.3 Spatial coherence structure of the currents

Our description of the spatio-temporal structure of the currents relies on empirical orthogonal functions (EOFs) and the spectral distribution of coherence (γ^2) and phase (ϕ). The EOFs partition variance of the current time series into coherent and independent (orthogonal) modes. They are, however, incapable of detecting propagating phenomena. Consequently, these are not appropriate techniques for detecting the along-slope structure in current variance if, for example, shelf waves and/or topographic Rossby waves are present in the data set (which we believe is true). Thus we restrict the EOF analyses to looking at the vertical structure of the currents and/or the cross-slope and vertical structure at the central and western moorings only. The EOFs computed on the correlation matrix, to ensure equal weighting of time series.

The coherence squared function, γ^2, quantifies the fraction of the variance in one time series that is correlated with the second series as a function of frequency (or period) while the phase function, ϕ, describes the phase relationship as a function of frequency for coherent signals. This spectral approach is appropriate for detecting propagating phenomena.

Table 5: Current statistics for Western Beaufort Moorings. Results from the principal axis decomposition are presented in terms of the variance explained (%) and orientation of the major axis (Θ_P), the integral time scale is τ, mean values for each velocity component V (cross-slope; north-south), U (along-slope; east-west) are in braces ("<>"), and the sample variance is denoted s^2. Italicized values of the velocity components indicated that these are significant at the 95% confidence level (from the student's t-test) after accounting for the integral time scale.

Mooring	Depth	Mean Velocity		Principal Axis		$|V|_{max}$	τ (days)	$<V>$	s^2_V	$<U>$	s^2_U
		Speed (cm s^{-1})	Θ_M	%	Θ_P	(cm s^{-1})		(cm s^{-1})	(cm s^{-1})^2	(cm s^{-1})	(cm s^{-1})^2
BFK_R1	72	8	115	95	114	31	2	-3.3	66	7.2	262
BFK_A1	82	7.1	107	95	113	64	2	-2.1	43	6.8	183
BFK_A2	86	7.5	107	94	114	65	2	-2.2	46	7.2	189
BFK_A3	90	6.7	107	94	114	64	2	-1.9	40	6.4	164
BFK_A4	94	5.6	106	94	114	62	2	-1.5	34	5.4	139
BFK_A5	98	4.6	105	94	113	60	2	-1.2	28	4.4	113
BFK_A6	102	3.6	102	93	112	62	2	-0.7	22	3.5	95
BFK_A7	106	2.6	97	92	111	68	2	-0.3	18	2.6	81
BFK_A8	110	1.5	83	91	108	72	2	0.2	13	1.5	63
BFK_A9	114	1.1	79	88	102	72	2	0.2	10	1	55
BFK_A10	118	0.8	86	85	96	64	2	0.1	8	0.8	42

Table 6: Record length current statistics for Central and Eastern Beaufort moorings.

Mooring	Depth	Mean Velocity			Principal Axis						
		Speed (cm s⁻¹)	Θ$_M$	%	Θ$_P$	$|V|_{max}$ (cm s⁻¹)	τ (days)	<V> (cm s⁻¹)	s^2_V (cm s⁻¹)²	<U> (cm s⁻¹)	s^2_U (cm s⁻¹)²
CENTRAL MOORINGS (B1, BFS, B3)											
B1 R2	72	6.6	91	95	99	59	3	-0.1	11	6.6	139
BFS R1	101	3.7	93	94	96	69	3.5	-0.2	29	3.7	414
BFS R2	192	5.8	103	96	92	80	6	-1.3	11	5.6	248
BFS R3	251	2.0	100	96	83	71	2	-0.3	5	1.9	84
BFS R4	413	2.7	105	93	98	40	2	-0.7	3	2.6	31
B3 R1	254	1.9	94	78	84	30	14	-0.1	11	1.9	37
B3 R2	355	1.5	105	82	80	18	12	-0.4	5.7	1.4	23
B3 R3	503	1.2	114	85	75	14	7	-0.5	3.7	1.1	15
EASTERN MOORING (B5)											
B5 R1	28	1.9	330	67	78	33	3	1.6	47	-0.9	90
B5 R2	128	1.9	174	62	61	43	9	-1.9	47	0.2	62
B5 R3	227	1.5	126	62	87	15	14	-0.9	4.6	1.2	7.4
B5 R4	476	1.2	112	87	101	12	11	-0.4	0.7	1.1	3.8

21

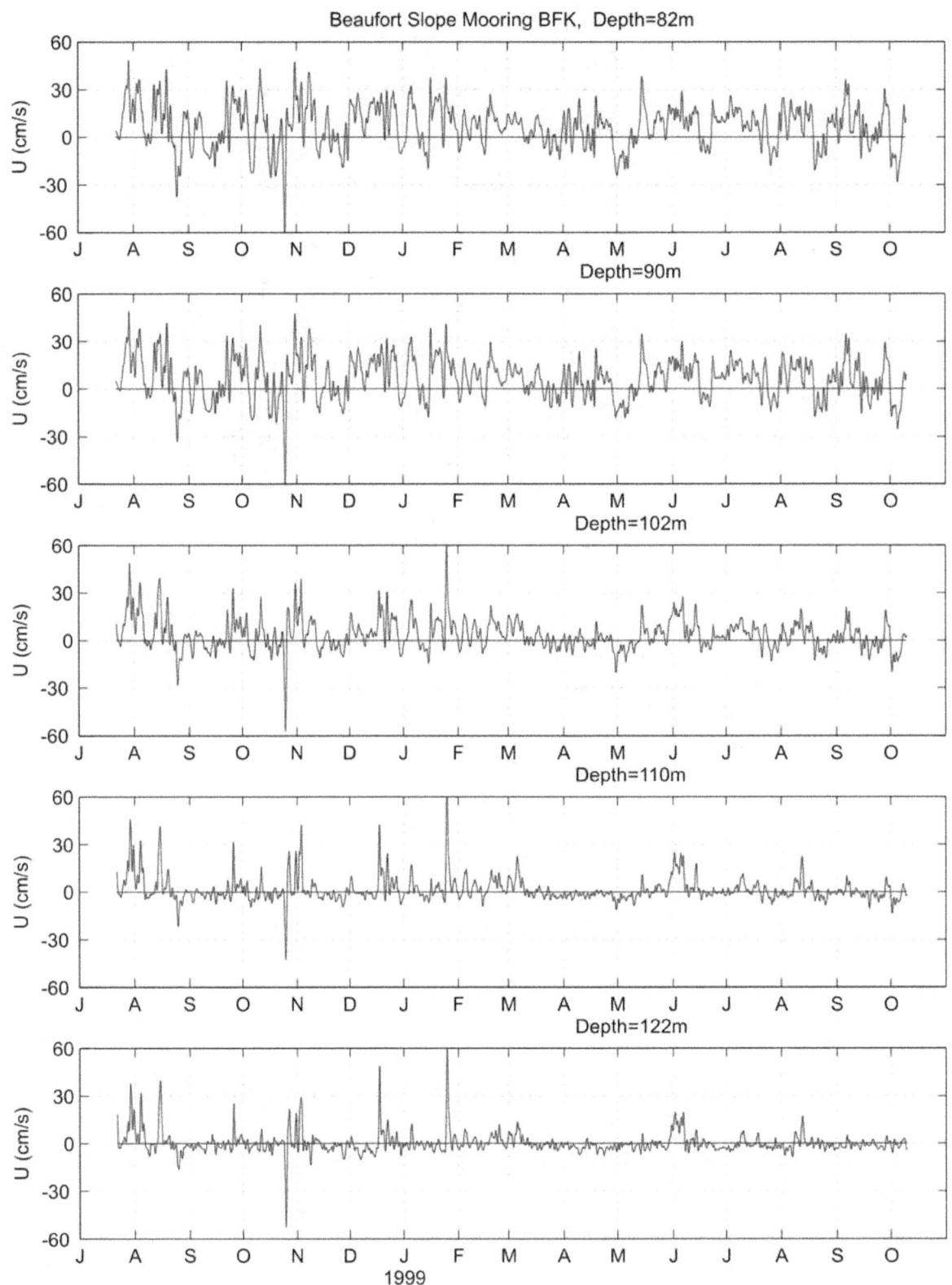

Figure 12: Along-slope (U) velocity at mooring BFK in the western Beaufort Sea.

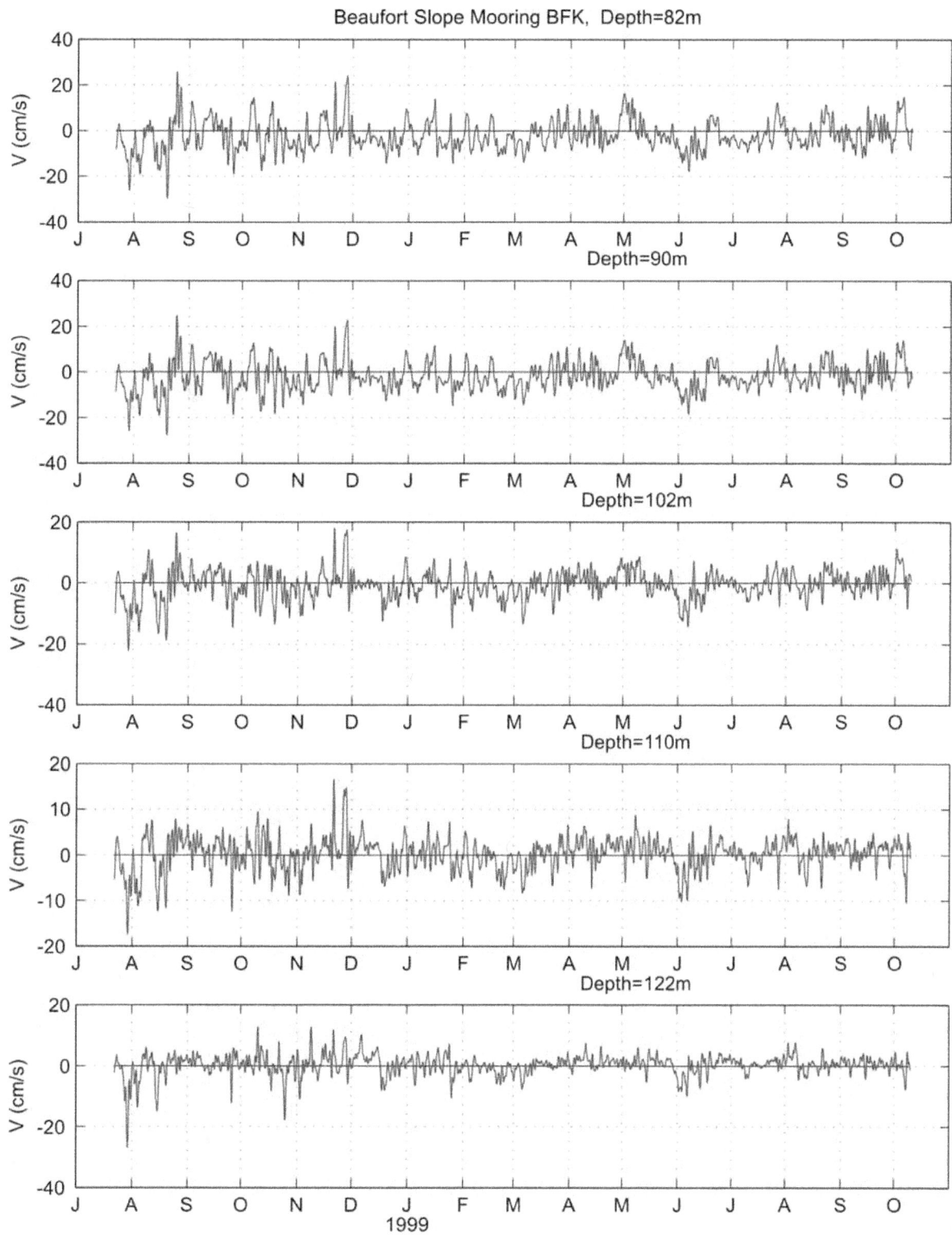

Figure 13: Cross-slope (V) velocity at mooring BFK in the western Beaufort Sea.

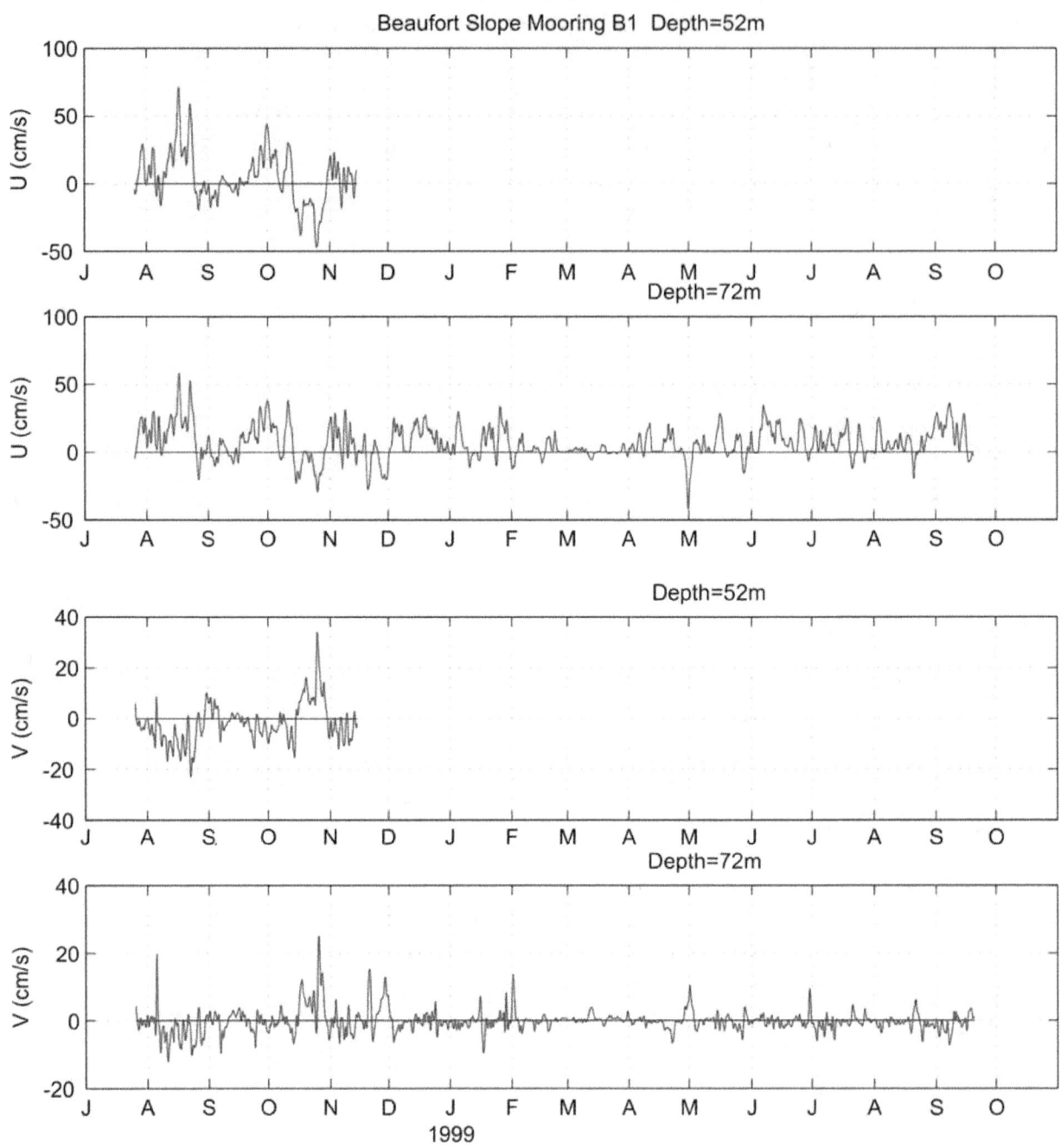

Figure 14: Along-slope (U) and cross-slope (V) velocities at mooring B1 in the central Beaufort Sea.

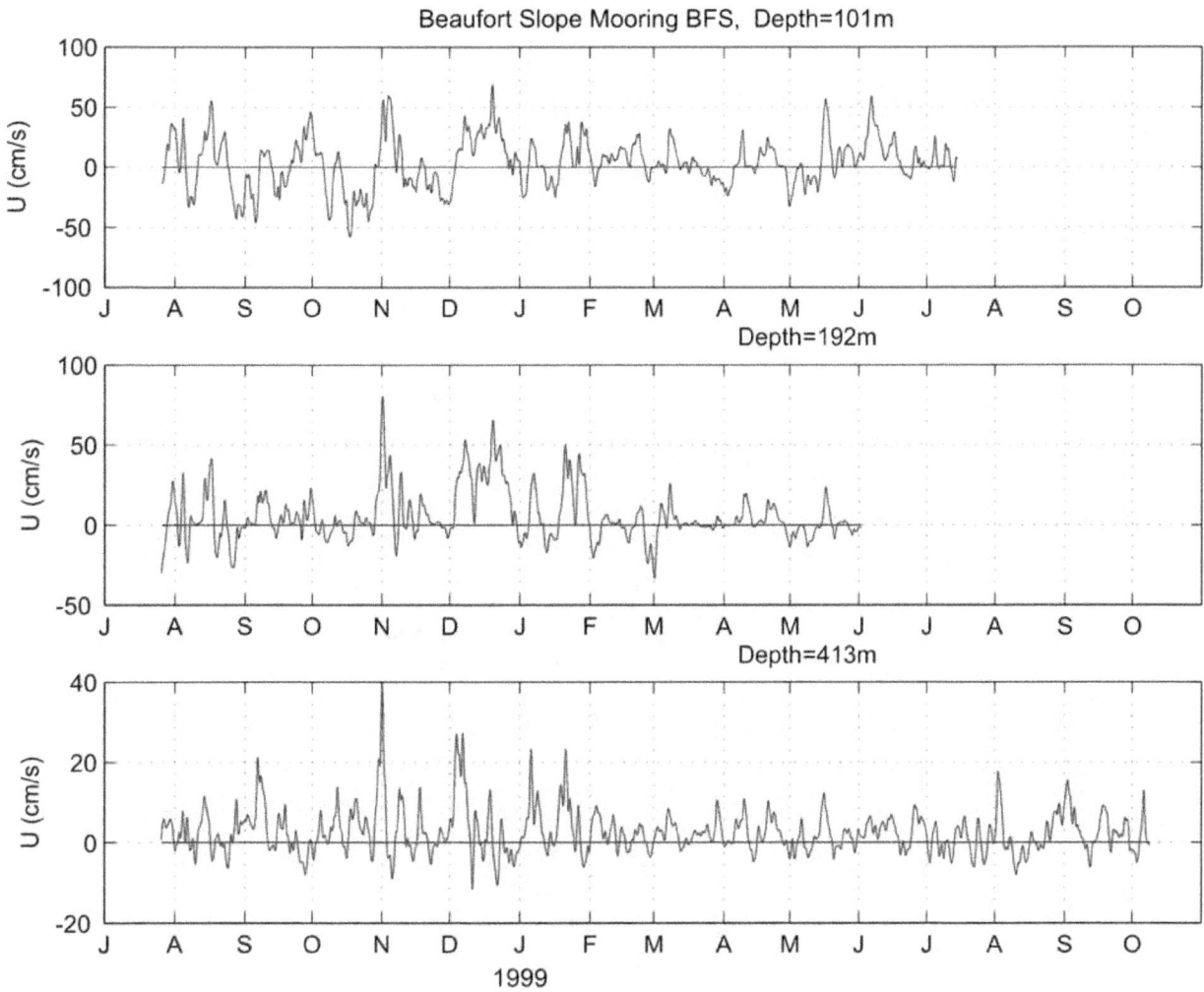

Figure 15: Along-slope (U) velocities at mooring BFS in the central Beaufort Sea.

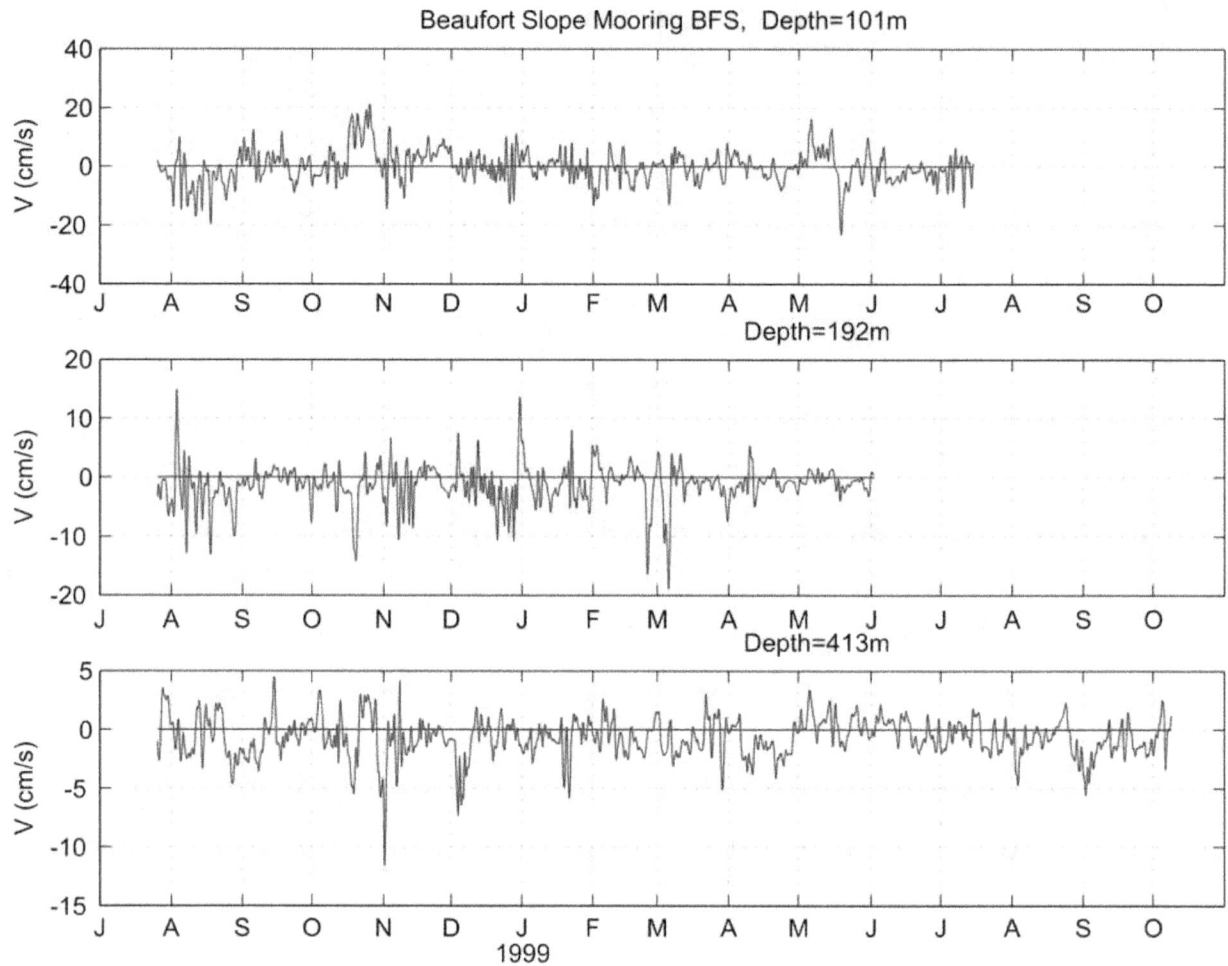

Figure 16: Cross-slope (V) velocities at mooring BFS in the central Beaufort Sea.

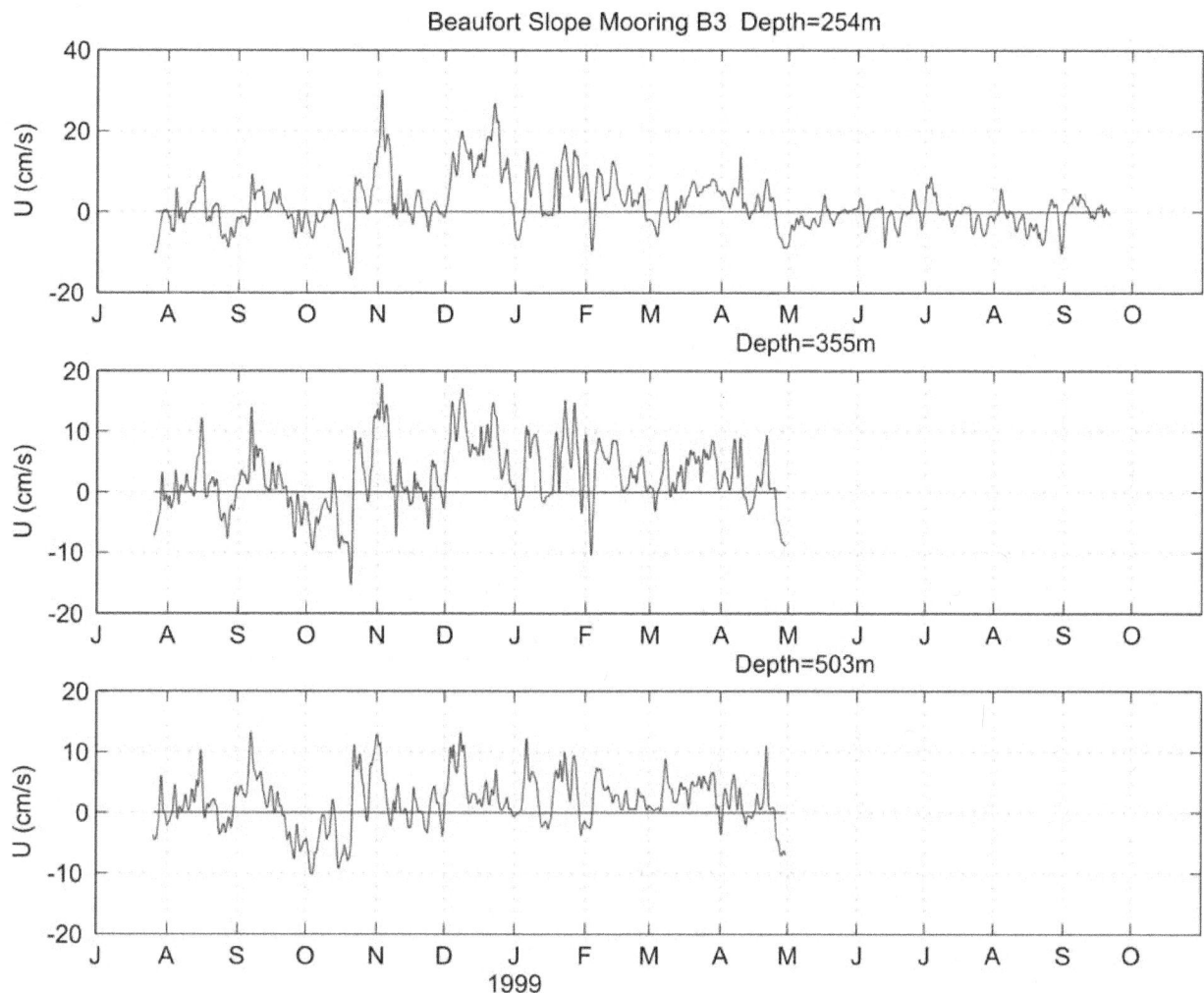

Figure 17: Along-slope (U) velocities at mooring B3 in the central Beaufort Sea.

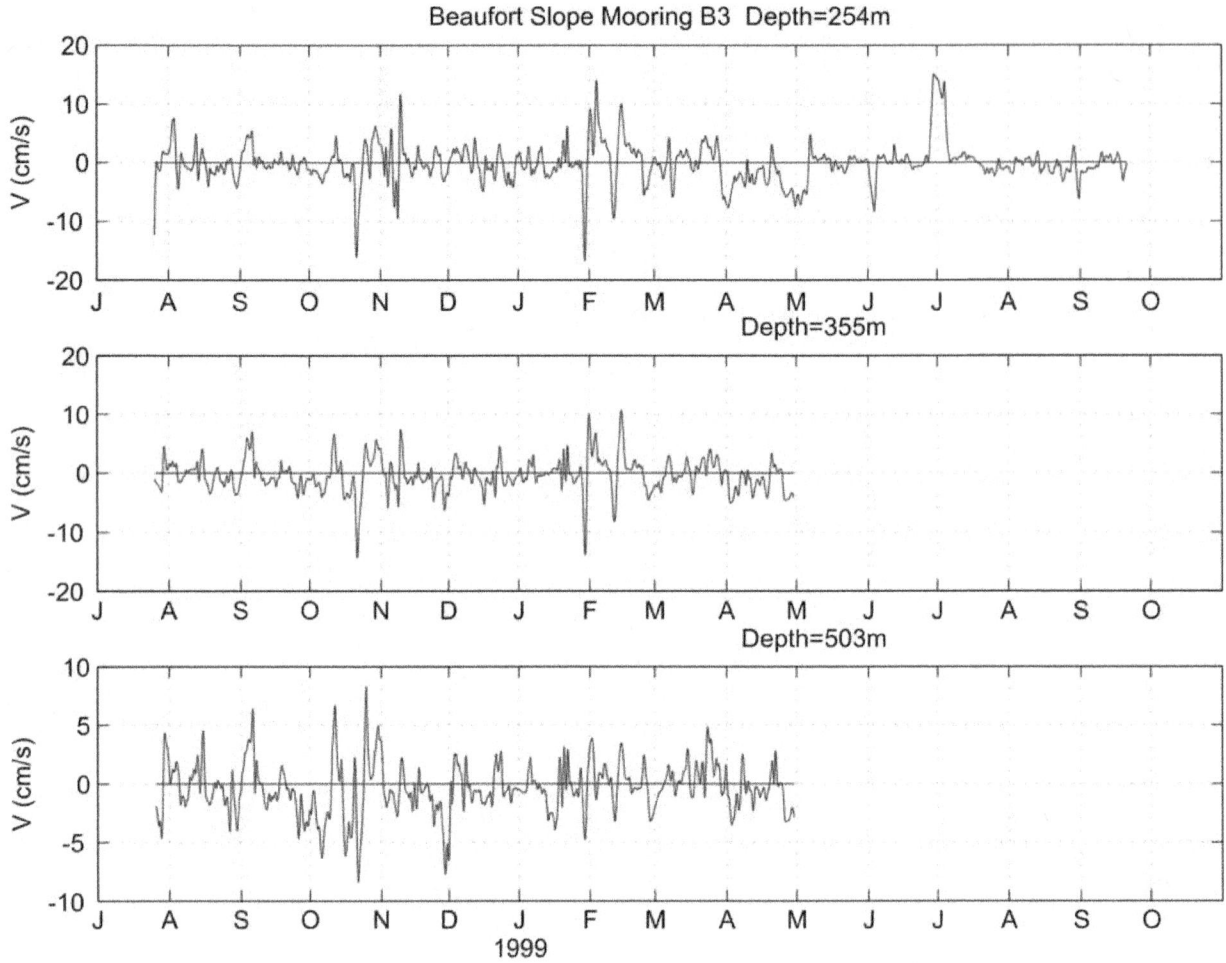

Figure 18: Cross-slope (V) velocities at mooring B3 in the central Beaufort Sea.

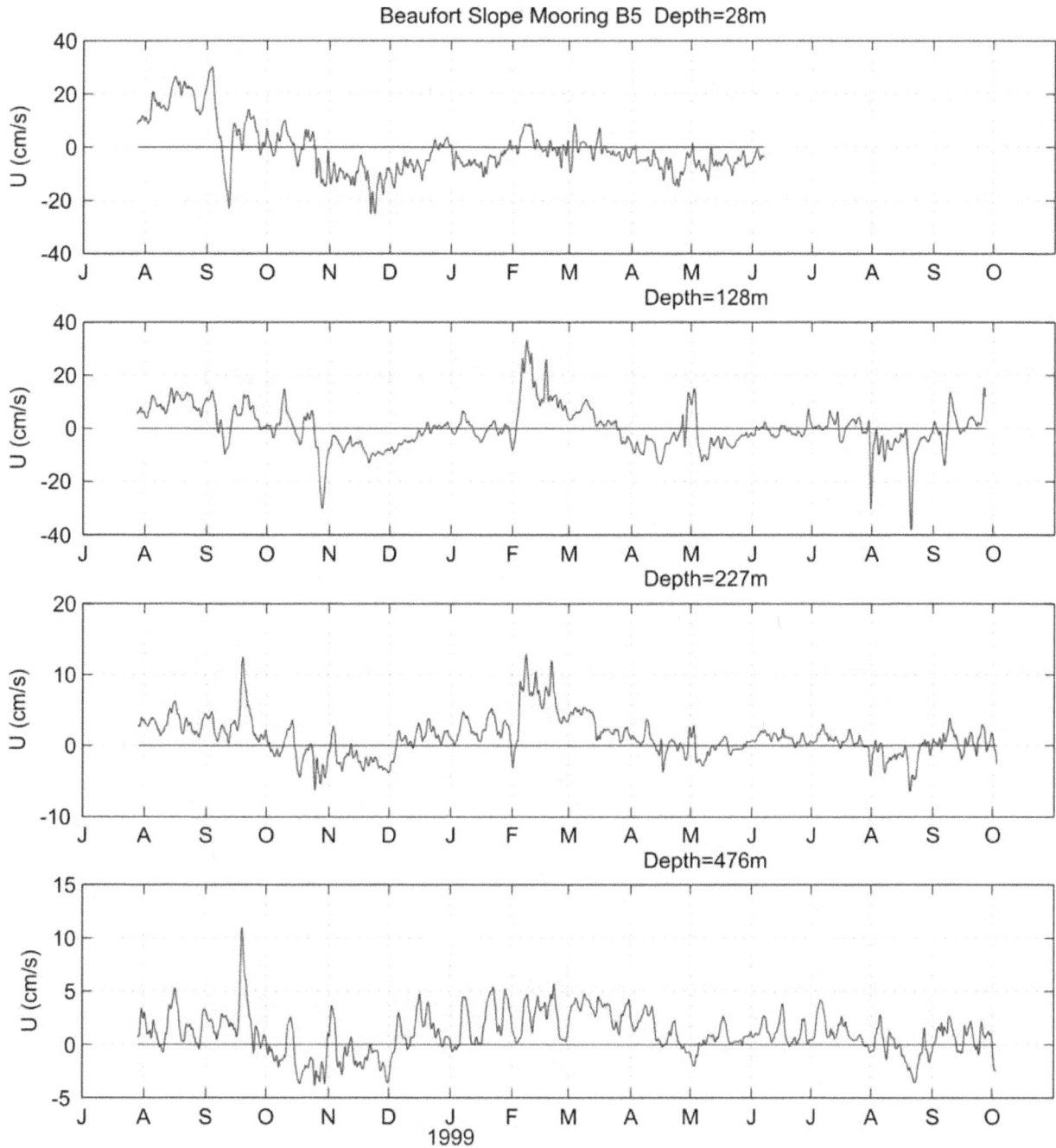

Figure 19: Along-slope (U) velocities at mooring B5 in the eastern Beaufort Sea.

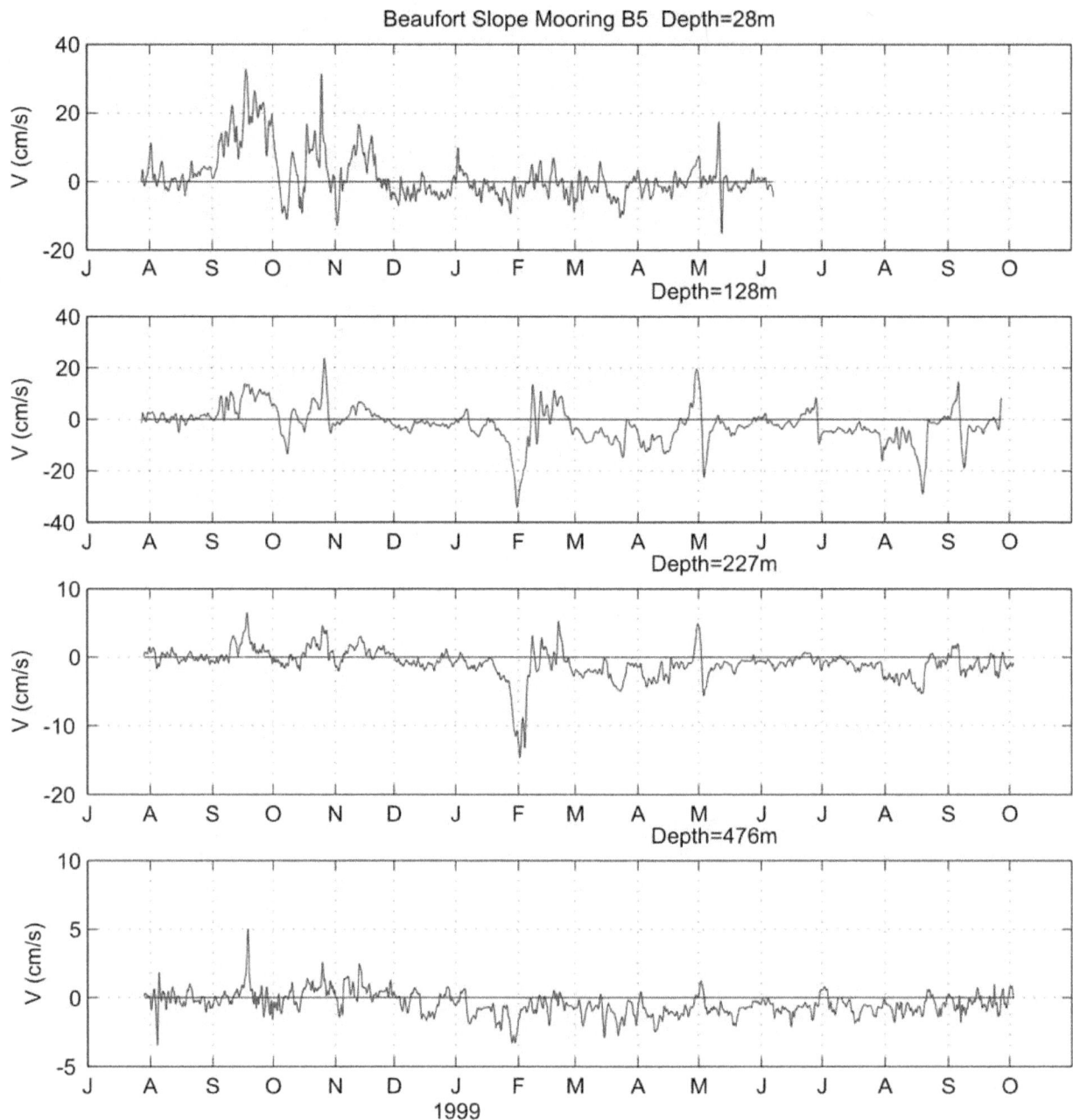

Figure 20: Cross-slope (V) velocities at mooring B5 in the eastern Beaufort Sea.

The EOF results for each velocity component for the eastern mooring (B5) are summarized in **Tables 7 and 8**. For the along-slope component only the first two modes are statistically significant by North's criterion and together these explain 90% of the variance. Mode 1 (69% of the variance) captures in-phase motions throughout the water column, but is most strongly correlated with the currents in the upper 227 m. Mode 2 (22% of the variance) is primarily correlated with currents at 28 m and 128 m depth. For the cross-slope component, Mode 1 captures 70% of the variance, with this mode once again projecting predominately on

the three uppermost depths. Mode 2 describes out-of-phase motions between the surface deeper meters, and correlates best with the cross-slope flow at 28 m. However, it is not significant by North's criterion. The EOF results for each velocity component for the central moorings (B1, BF_S, and B3) are listed in **Tables 9 and 10**. For the along-slope component only the first mode is statistically significant. It indicates that ~55% of the along- slope current variance is in-phase in the vertical and across the slope. The correlations between

Table 7: EOF results for the along-slope velocity components at the eastern Beaufort mooring (B5). The entries in the first four rows of the table are the correlation between the original data and the mode. The last row lists the percent variance explained by a given mode.

Mooring	Depth (m)	Mode 1	Mode 2
B5_R1	28	0.86	-0.97
B5_R2	128	0.94	-0.75
B5_R3	227	0.82	-0.41
B5_R4	476	0.54	-0.09
%Variance explained		68.71	21.81

Table 8: Except for the EOF results for the cross-slope velocity components at the eastern Beaufort mooring (B5). The entries in the first four rows of the table are the correlation between the original data and the mode. The last row lists the percent variance explained by a given mode.

Mooring	Depth (m)	Mode 1	Mode 2
B5_R1	28	0.84	0.99
B5_R2	128	0.94	0.62
B5_R3	227	0.85	0.44
B5_R4	476	0.62	0.35
%Variance explained		70.4	14.6

Table 9: EOF results for the along-slope velocity components at the central mooring (B1, BF_S, B4). The entries in the first four rows of the table are the correlation between the original data and the mode. The last row lists the percent variance explained by a given mode.

Mooring	Depth (m)	Mode 1	Mode 2
B1_R2	72	0.60	-0.83
BFS_R1	101	0.86	-0.91
BFS_R2	192	0.90	-0.62
BFS_R4	413	0.37	0.03
B3_R1	254	0.81	-0.37
B3_R2	355	0.76	-0.23
B3_R3	503	0.61	-0.04
%Variance explained		55.4	19.8

Table 10: EOF results for the along-slope velocity components at the central mooring (B1, BF_S, B4). The entries in the first four rows of the table are the correlation between the original data and the mode. The last row lists the percent variance explained by a given mode.

Mooring	Depth (m)	Mode 1	Mode 2
B1_R2	72	-0.25	-0.72
BFS_R1	101	-0.25	-0.89
BFS_R2	192	0.29	-0.45
BFS_R4	413	-0.16	-0.11
B3_R1	254	0.89	-0.13
B3_R2	355	0.93	-0.02
B3_R3	503	0.81	0.04
%Variance explained		36.7	22.3

this mode and the original data are largest at depths less than 250 m indicating that this mode primarily projects onto the shallower currents. Mode 2 (20% of the variance) largely captures variance in the shallow meters closest to the shelfbreak. The other modes (not shown) are not significant, and generally correlate with only one or two depths. For the cross-slope component, Mode 1 captures 70% of the variance, with this mode once again projecting predominately on the three uppermost meters. Mode 2 describes out-of-phase motions between the surface deeper meters, and correlates best with the cross-slope flow at 28 m. However, it is not significant by North's criterion. The cross-slope velocity component has a complicated structure with the first mode (37% of the variance) primarily correlated with mooring B3 and the second mode projecting onto the shallow instruments at moorings B1 and BF_S.

Overall, the EOF analysis indicates a complicated vertical and cross-slope velocity structure over the central Beaufort slope as the variance is broadly distributed over a number of modes that are not well resolved. This further suggests that the sampling design (in terms of numbers of instruments and cross-slope distribution and/or record lengths) was insufficient to adequately describe the horizontal and vertical resolution of our instruments. On the other hand the result for the eastern mooring

(B5) suggests a relatively simple current pattern in the vertical, with most of the current variance accounted for by the 1st mode (e.g., the currents over the uppermost 500 m coherent) and the 2nd mode capturing the near surface variability.

We next consider the results from the coherence analysis. **Figure 21** reveals that the along-slope currents at the shelfbreak between the western (BFK) and central Beaufort Sea (B1) are generally coherent at periods between 72 and 240 hours (3 – 10 days) and at periods > 18 days. At shorter periods the phase is negative (when γ^2 exceeds the 95% significance level) indicating eastward phase propagation. For example, at periods of ~6 days, the phase lag is about 1 day, suggesting that current events at this period are propagating eastward at a phase speed of ~2.3 m s^{-1}. For periods > 18 days currents are in-phase. In contrast, the along-slope currents between B1 and B5 are incoherent (not shown) and coherence is small between the deeper currents at either BFS or B3 and B5 (**Figures 22** and **23**).

IV. 4 Wind-current relationships

Figures 24 – 28 summarize the correlation (in terms of γ^2 and ϕ) between along-slope winds (using Barrow winds) and along-slope currents for several of the moorings. (Similar results were obtained using the ECMWF winds.) Winds and currents are coherent for the shelfbreak moorings in the western (BFK; **Figure 24**) and central (B1) Beaufort Sea (**Figure 25**) and for the currents at 101 m at mooring BFS (**Figure 26**). However, the wind-current coherence is stronger at shorter periods (< 0 days) over the western slope than over the central slope. Winds and along-slope currents are generally incoherent for depths > 100 m for the central moorings (BFS or B3; not shown) or in the western Beaufort Sea (B5 at 28 m; **Figure 27** and at 128 m; **Figure 28**).

The statistical analyses suggests that the along-slope currents at the shelfbreak (BFK and B1) have an along-slope correlation scale of at least 200 km, but that seaward of the shelfbreak and for depths ±100 m, the along-slope correlation scale is < 200 km. Caution should be

exercised in assuming that these scales hold along the entire Beaufort slope, however. For example the bathymetric slope in the eastern Beaufort Sea is much gentler than in the central and western Beaufort and mooring B5 is further seaward of the shelfbreak than the moorings to the west. Indeed, mooring B5 might not have been deployed in the undercurrent and so current fluctuations here might not be representative of undercurrent variability closer to the shelfbreak. In addition, we show in the next section that the along-slope density gradient changes between the eastern and western Beaufort slope. This will alter the dynamics governing the undercurrent and degrade the correlation between the eastern and central Beaufort slope.

The wind-current relationship also weakens, moving eastward along the slope and deeper into the water column. The latter result may suggest that deep ocean motion forces remotely dominate the subsurface current variations. The lack of a coherent response at shallower depths at the central and eastern mooring sites is harder to understand, however. While these sites may also be responding to deeper ocean dynamics that are unrelated to local wind stress, the reduction in coherence might be associated with variations in the regional ice conditions. Analysis of 10-day repeat Synthetic Aperture Radar (SAR) imagery by A. Mahoney and H. Eicken (pers. communication) indicates that the pack ice was immobile over the eastern and central Beaufort slope for at least 30 days (and possibly longer) in April 1999, whereas highly mobile pack ice covered the western Beaufort slope. The differences in ice mobility should result in along-slope variations in the surface stress, which would degrade the coherence. Mahoney and Eicken show that similar ice conditions occurred in the winter of 2000, while in the five other years they examined freely drifting pack ice extended along the entire Beaufort slope. This issue deserves theoretical attention because it implies that the wind-current response and slope flows could vary substantially between years.

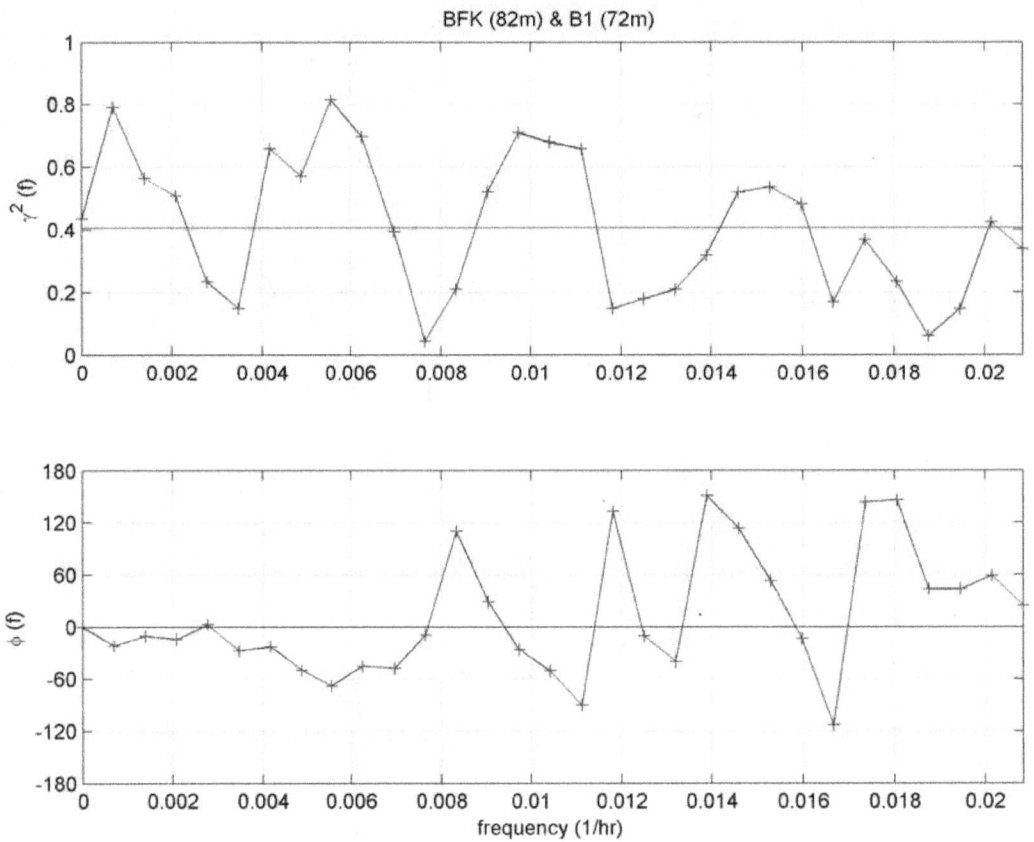

Figure 21: Coherence squared (γ^2; upper panel) and phase (ϕ; lower panel) as a function of frequency for the along-slope currents at BFK (western Beaufort Sea) and B1 (central Beaufort Sea). The horizontal red line on the γ^2 plot indicates the 95% significance level for γ^2.

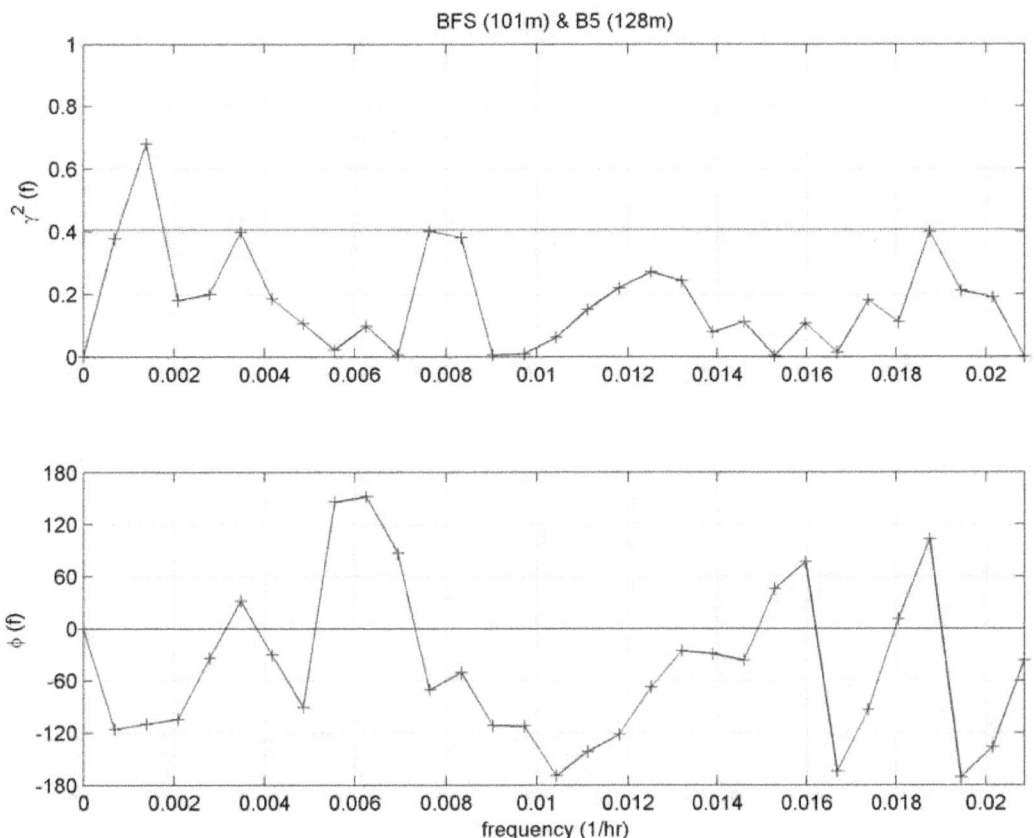

Figure 22: Coherence squared (γ^2; upper panel) and phase (ϕ; lower panel) as a function of frequency for the along-slope currents at 101 m at BFS (central Beaufort Sea) and at 128 m at B5 (eastern Beaufort Sea). The horizontal red line on the γ^2 plot indicates the 95% significance level for γ^2.

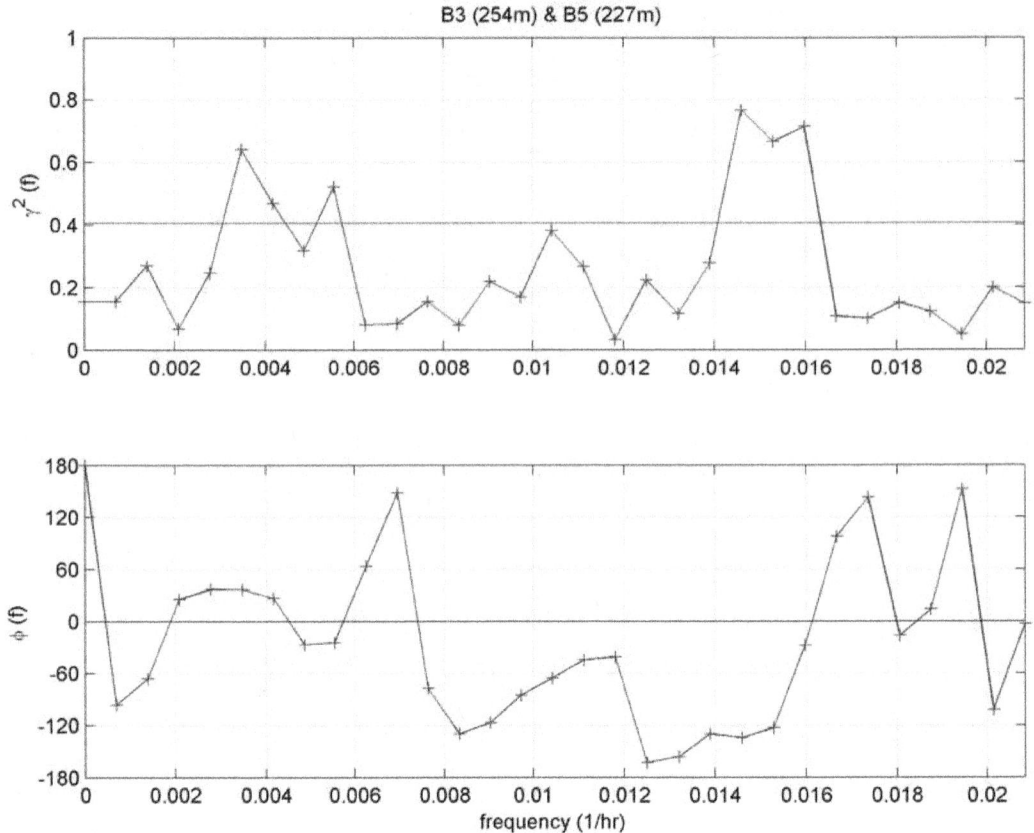

Figure 23: Coherence squared (γ^2; upper panel) and phase (ϕ; lower panel) as a function of frequency for the along-slope currents at 254 m at B3 (central Beaufort Sea) and at 227 m at B5 (eastern Beaufort Sea). The horizontal red line on the γ^2 plot indicates the 95% significance level for γ^2.

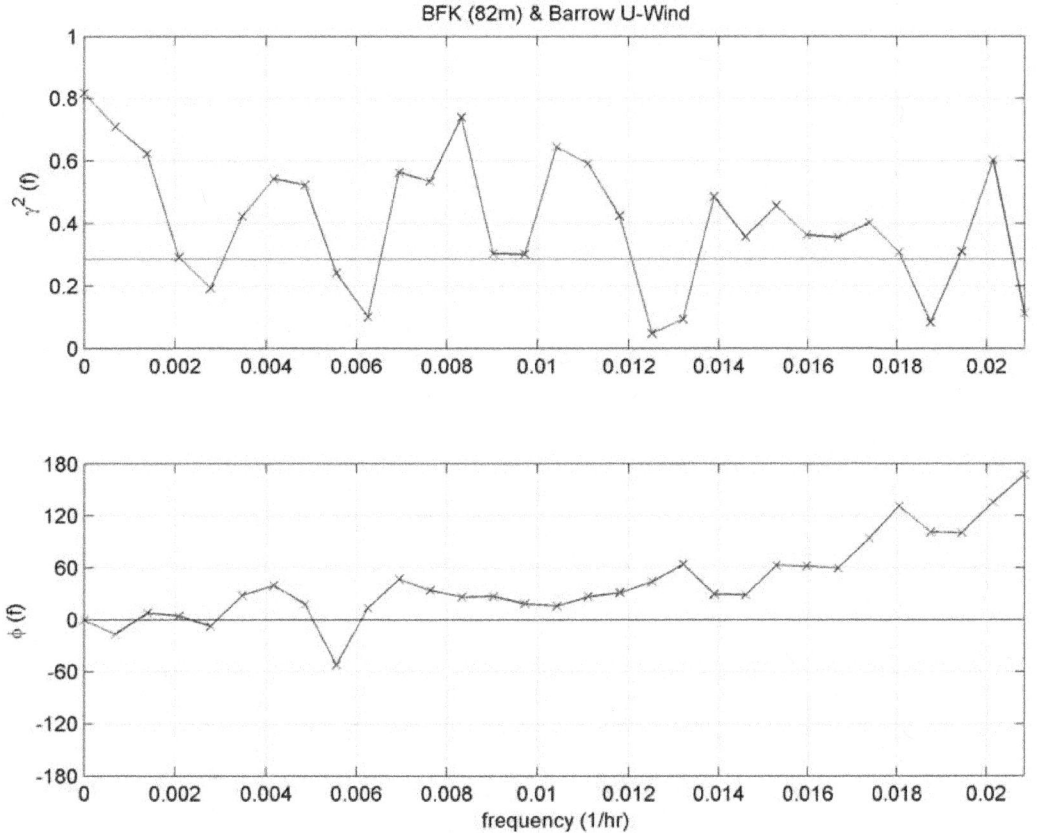

Figure 24: Coherence squared (γ^2; upper panel) and phase (ϕ; lower panel) as a function of frequency for the along-slope currents at BFK (western Beaufort Sea) and along-slope winds at Barrow. The horizontal red line on the γ^2 plot indicates the 95% significance level for γ^2.

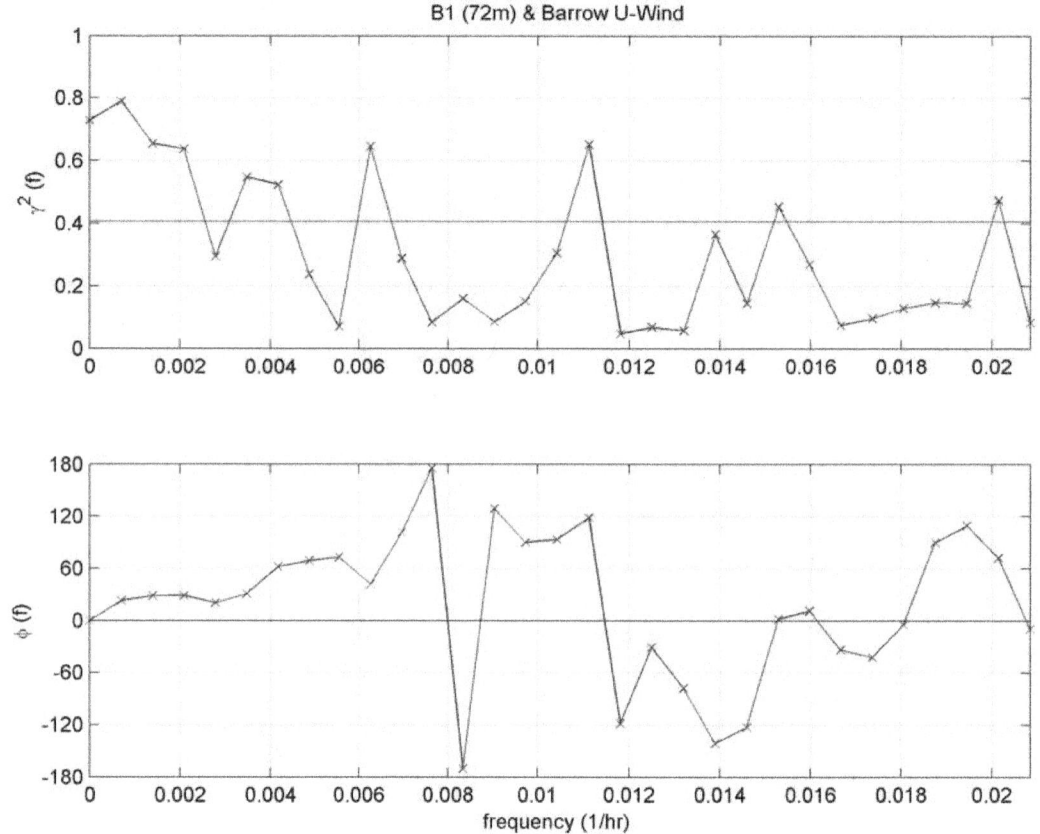

Figure 25: Coherence squared (γ^2; upper panel) and phase (ϕ; lower panel) as a function of frequency for the along-slope currents at B1, 72 m (central Beaufort Sea) and along-slope winds at Barrow. The horizontal red line on the γ^2 plot indicates the 95% significance level for γ^2.

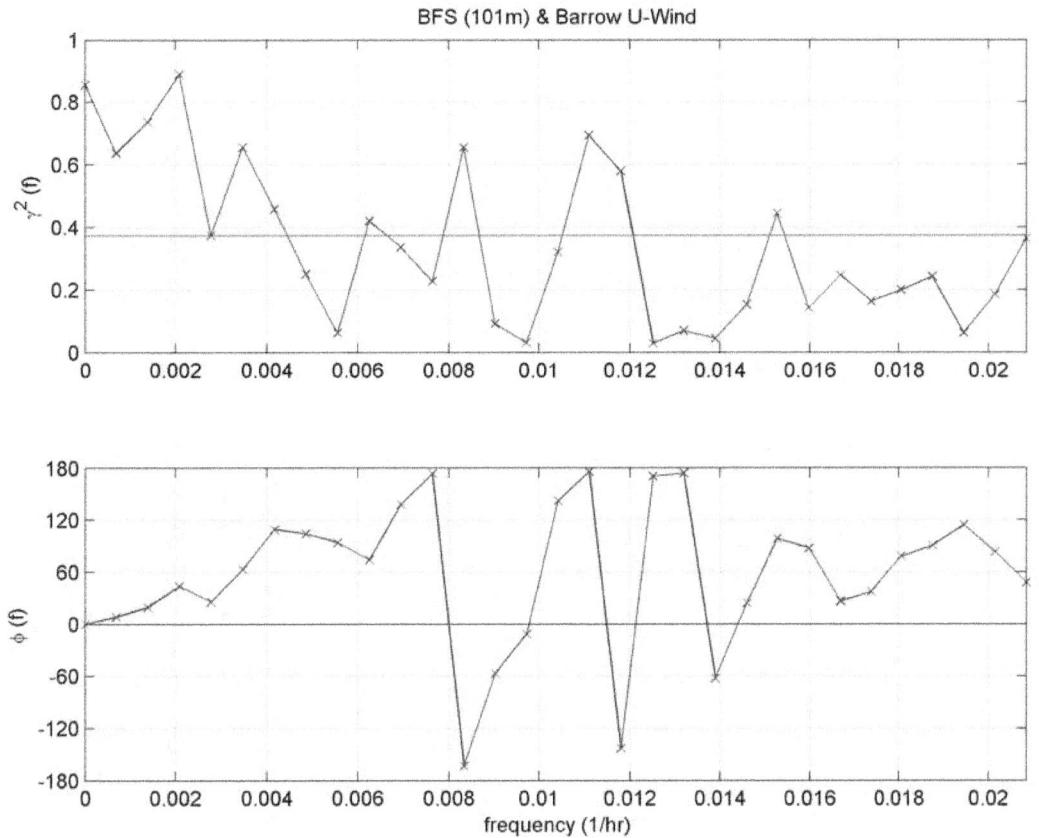

Figure 26: Coherence squared (γ^2; upper panel) and phase (ϕ; lower panel) as a function of frequency for the along-slope currents at BF_S, 101 m (central Beaufort Sea) and along-slope winds at Barrow. The horizontal red line on the γ^2 plot indicates the 95% significance level for γ^2.

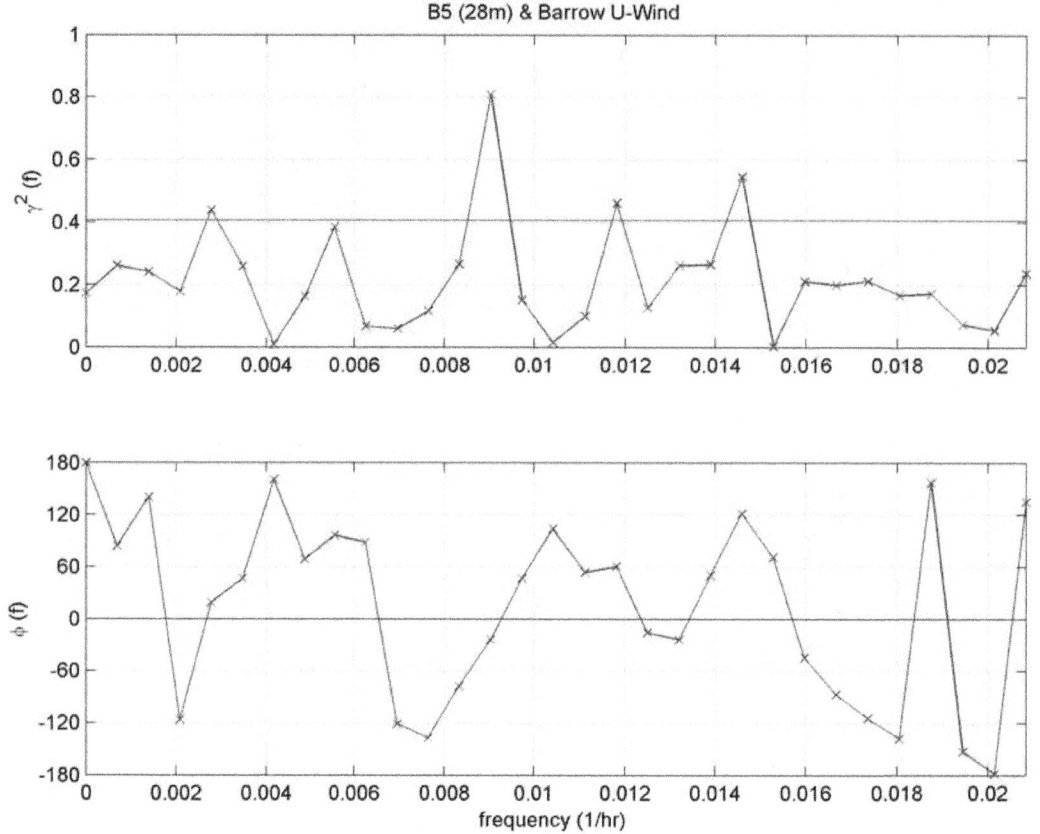

Figure 27: Coherence squared (γ^2; upper panel) and phase (ϕ; lower panel) as a function of frequency for the along-slope currents at B5, 28 m (eastern Beaufort Sea) and along-slope winds at Barrow. The horizontal red line on the γ^2 plot indicates the 95% significance level for γ^2.

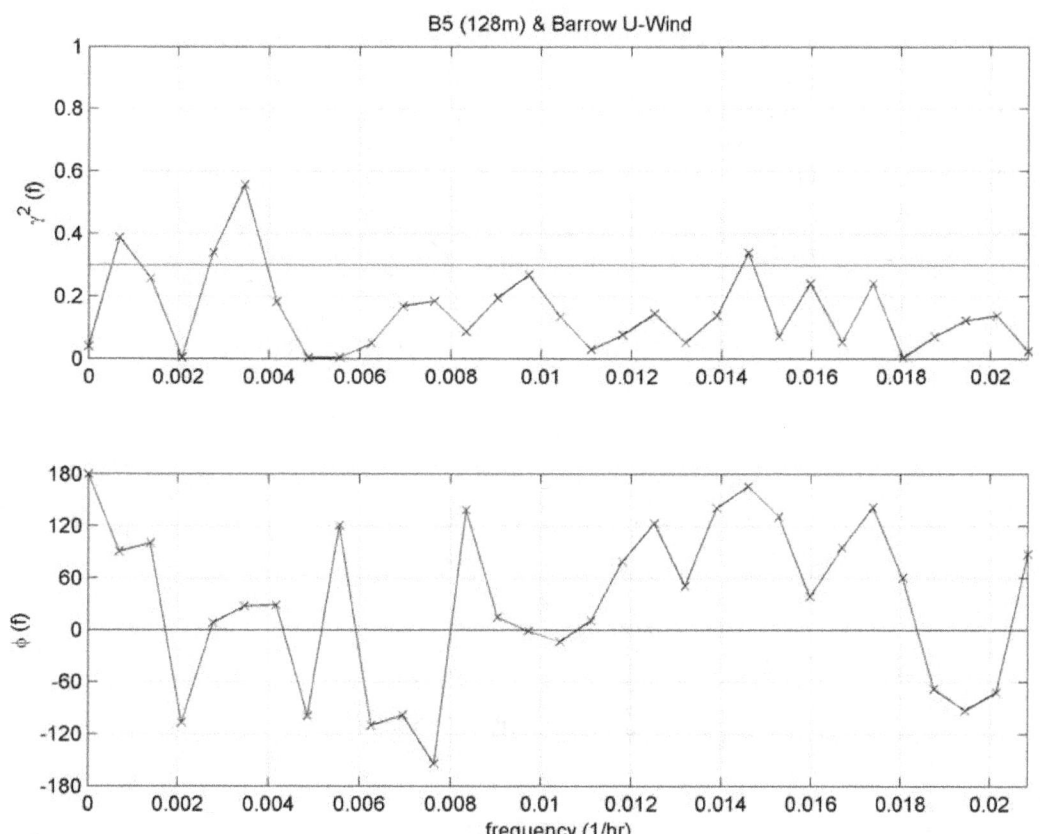

Figure 28: Coherence squared (γ^2; upper panel) and phase (ϕ; lower panel) as a function of frequency for the along-slope currents at B5, 128 m (eastern Beaufort Sea) and along-slope winds at Barrow. The horizontal red line on the γ^2 plot indicates the 95% significance level for γ^2.

IV. 5 Temperature and Salinity variability

There are four broad water mass classes observed at the moorings, of which three are shown in **Figure 29**. Bering Sea Summer Water, which occurs above the halocline has temperatures > 0°C and salinities ±32.2. Winter–Modified Shelf Water, occupies the upper halocline and has temperatures at or near the freezing point and a salinity range of 32 – 33.1. Atlantic-Modified Water occupies the lower halocline with a temperature range of -1.5°C to 0.5°C and salinities > 33.1. The fourth water mass, observed only at mooring B5 at 28 m depth (**Figure 33**), is Arctic Ocean mixed layer water (salinities < 31.2 and temperatures generally < 0°C). With this classification and the vertical profiles of temperature and salinity shown in **Figure 6** as guides, the time series plots of temperature and salinity from each instrument (**Figures 30 – 33**) are more

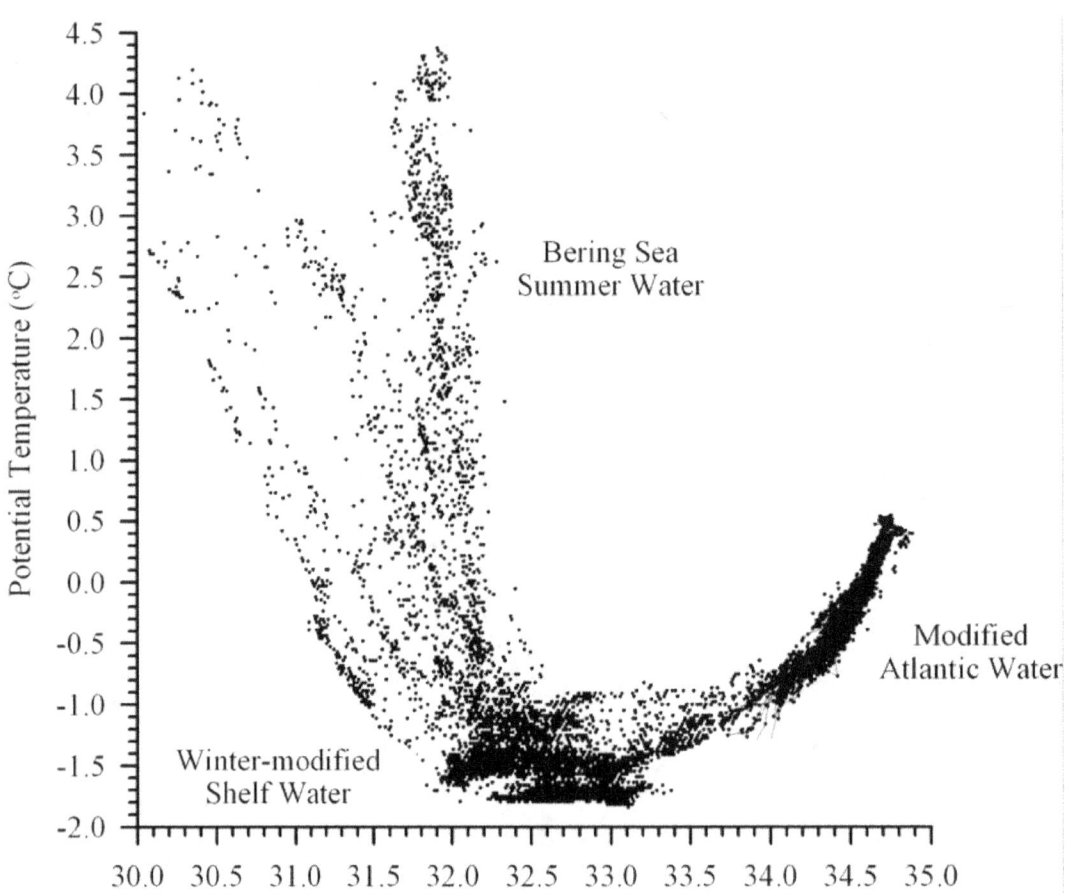

Figure 29: Potential temperature-salinity diagram describing water mass nomenclature for waters observed at depths ≤250m.

easily understood. These show considerable complexity and variability among sites, although several general conclusions can be drawn. First, the warmer fractions of Bering Sea Summer Water are only observed at the western (BFK) and central (B1) shelfbreak moorings at depths < 73 m. Although present at BFK in August 1998 and August – September 1999, it occurred at B1 only in September 1999. It appeared at B1 approximately 30 days after its first appearance at BFK in August 1999, with this time difference consistent with the mean flow along the shelfbreak being 6 – 7 cm s^{-1}. There are also several prominent upwelling events in which Modified Atlantic Water was upwelled. These events appear as rapid increases in both temperature and salinity at BFK (104 and 116 m; **Figure 30**) and at mooring BFS (101 and 133 m; **Figure 31**) in October and late November – December 1998 and April and May 1999 and are most likely related to the strong upwelling-favorable wind pulses during these months. While the fall 1998 upwelling signals are evident in the shelfbreak moorings (BFK and B1), they are not reflected at 73 m depth at mooring BFS (**Figure 32**), which is seaward of the shelfbreak. This suggests that upwelling into the near-surface layer is stronger at the shelfbreak than further offshore. If we assume that the temperature change at 133 m at mooring BFS in October is solely due to upwelling (no horizontal advection and/or mixing) then the vertical velocity was ~4.5 m/day at this location. These are relatively large vertical velocities, being comparable to the vertical velocities observed during moderately strong upwelling events on mid-latitude shelves.

The upwelling episodes discussed above are associated with very low-frequency displacements of the lower halocline (water depths > 190 m) evident at moorings BFS and B3. For example, at mooring BFS the lower halocline waters upwelled from September – November, 1999, March – May 1999 and August – September 1999, when westward wind stress was greatest. The downwelling periods of December 1998 – January 1999 and June – July 1999 were associated with westward winds (December – January) or relaxation in westward wind stress (June – July). We note, however that we do not find any consistent relationship between upwelling of the undercurrent and along-shelf currents at the shelfbreak. During some upwelling events the shelfbreak currents accelerate eastward (suggesting vertical advection of eastward momentum) while other events are associated with westward acceleration.

Temperature and salinity variations over the eastern Beaufort slope (mooring B5; **Figure 34**) differ substantially from those to the east. For example, both the high and low-frequency vertical displacements of the halocline are largely suppressed throughout the record. The reason for this is not at all clear, for even in the absence of a local wind stress we might have expected substantial halocline variability in the eastern Beaufort Sea due to eastward propagating topographic waves. The SeaCat record at 28 m shows no evidence of upwelling or Bering Sea Summer Water. The principle seasonal transitions at 28 m are the rapid cooling (from 0°C to -1.5°C) and freshening (from 32.3 to 28.5) that began in late November 1998 and continued through January 1999 followed by a rapid salinity increase in February. These transitions appear to be associated with horizontal advection. The cooling and freshening event occurred during a period of strong westward flow, whereas the salinity increase occurred in conjunction with southeastward flow.

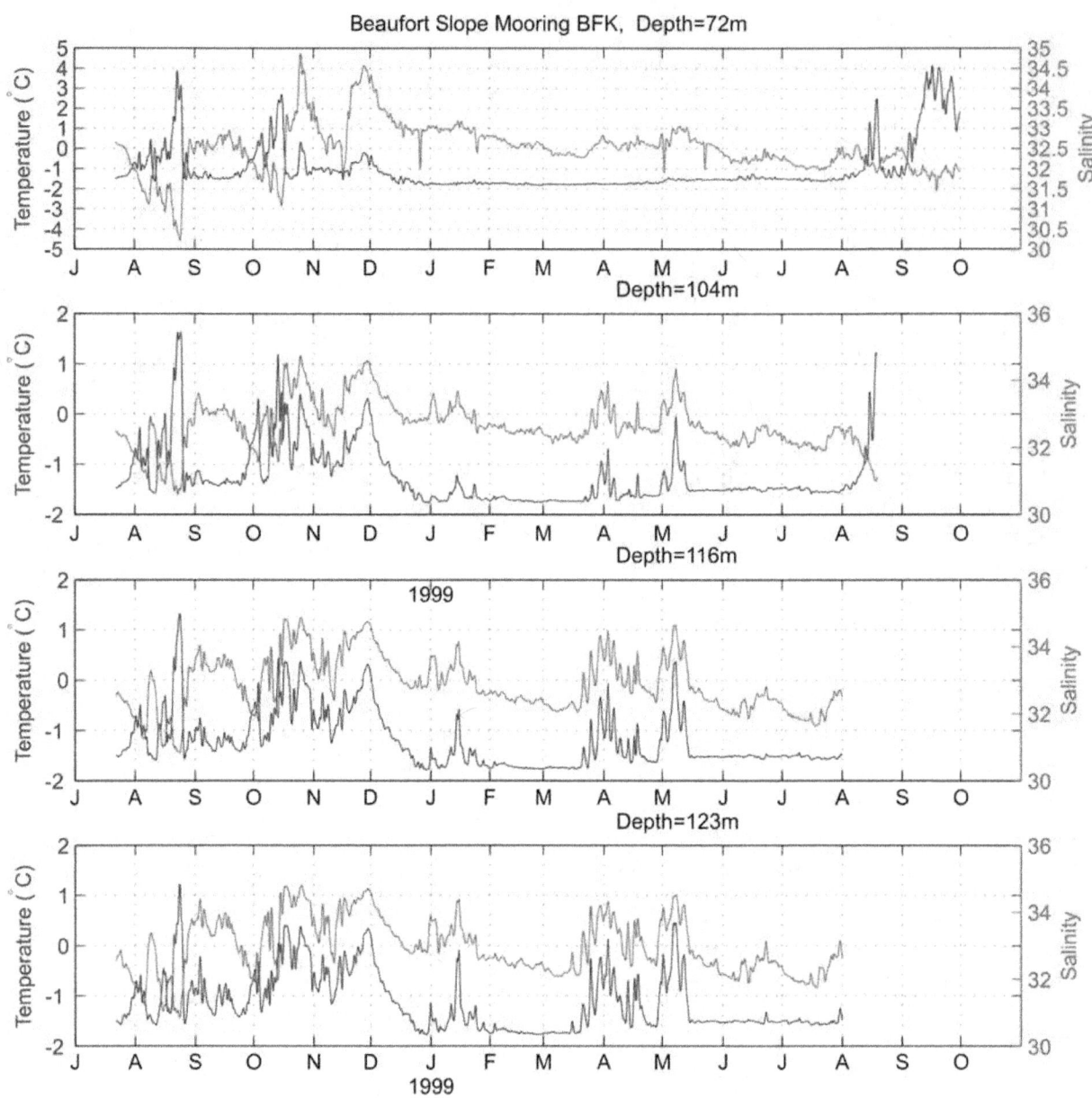

Figure 30: Temperature and salinity at mooring BFK in the western Beaufort Sea.

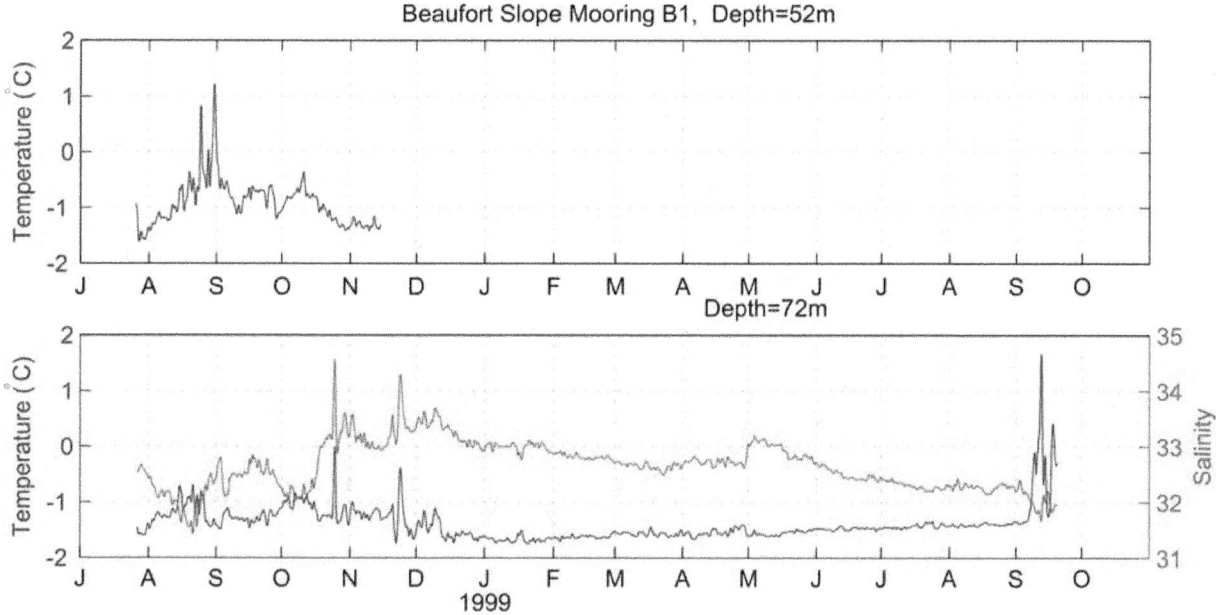

Figure 31: Temperature and salinity at mooring B1 in the central Beaufort Sea. (No salinity data at 52 m depth.)

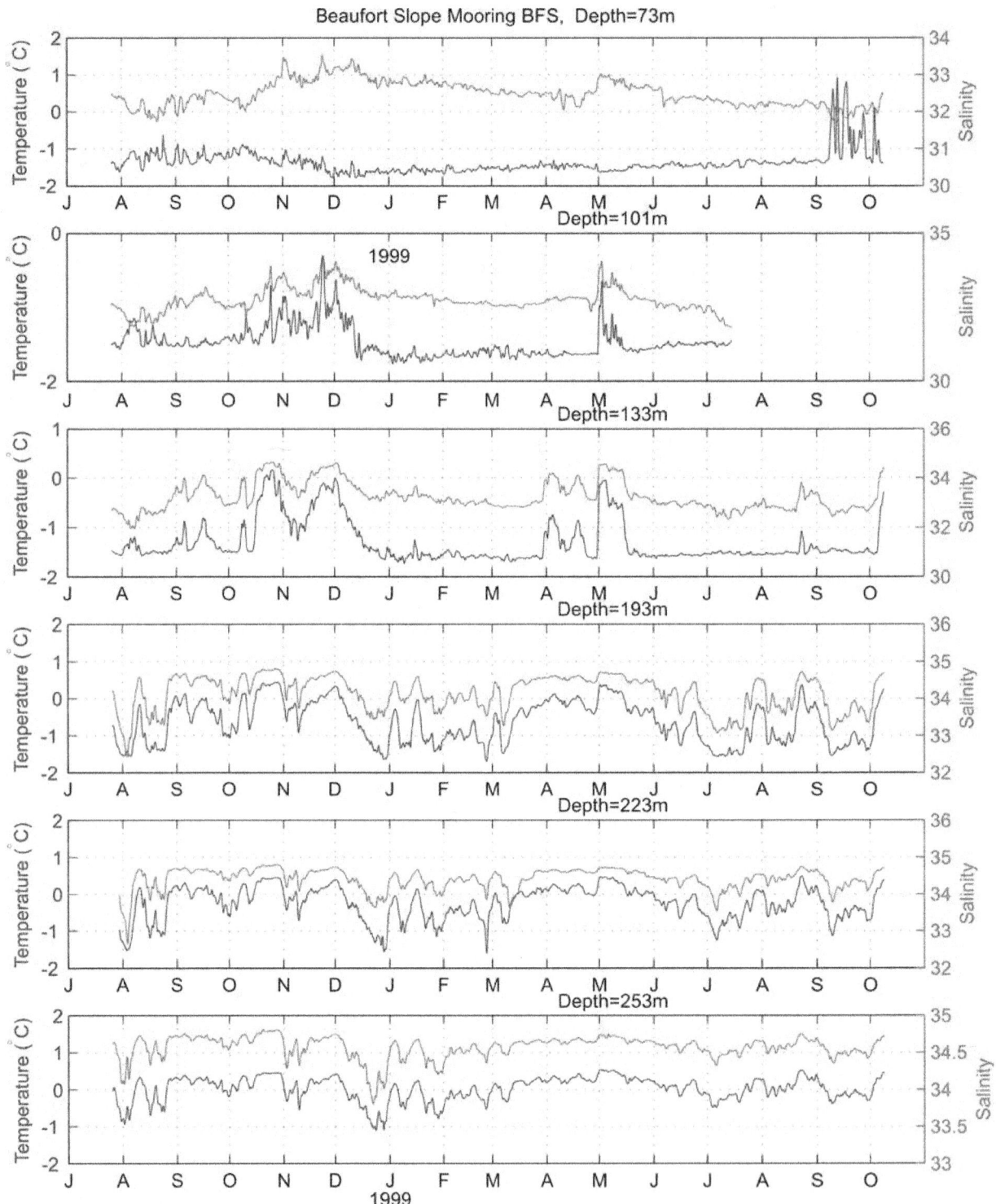

Figure 32: Temperature and salinity at mooring BFS in the central Beaufort Sea.

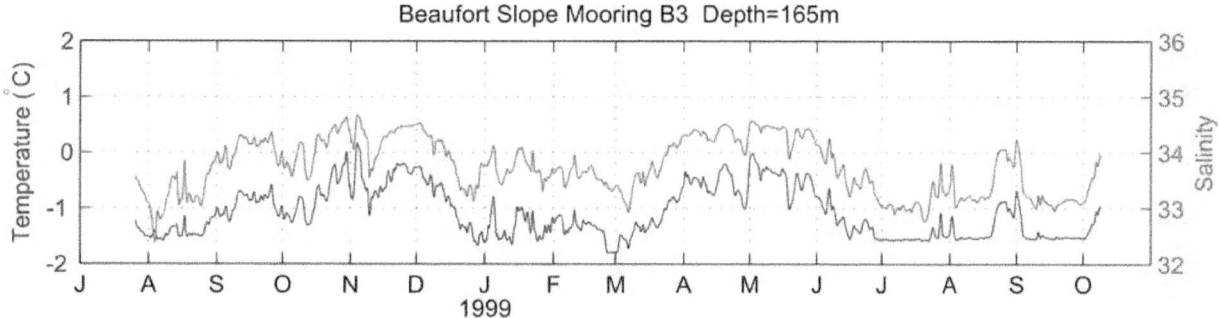

Figure 33: Temperature and salinity at mooring B3 in the central Beaufort Sea.

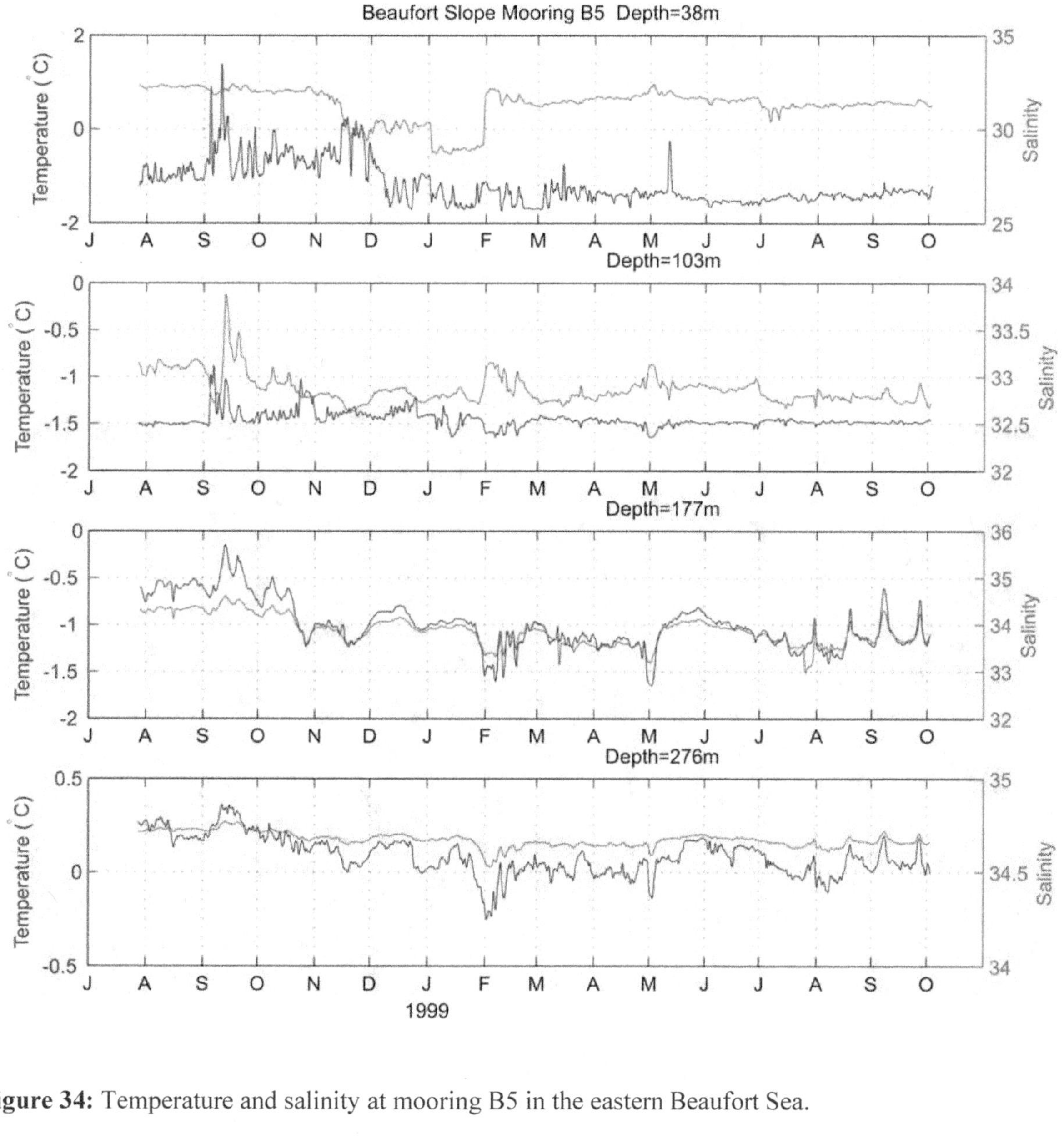

Beaufort Slope Mooring B5 Depth=38m

Depth=103m

Depth=177m

Depth=276m

1999

Figure 34: Temperature and salinity at mooring B5 in the eastern Beaufort Sea.

IV.6 Submarine Hydrography

Submarine hydrographic data are used to illustrate the along-slope thermohaline (and density) structure, which is an important component in the dynamics of the along-slope flow. **Figure 35** shows the along-slope temperature and salinity structure collected by the temperature-conductivity recorder in the submarine sail during transit along the slope. The measurements were made in the upper halocline at 117 m ($\pm$ 1 m) depth between longitudes 159°W (eastern end of the Chukchi Sea slope) and 142°W (eastern end of the Beaufort Sea slope). Two prominent spatial scales of variability are evident. The short-scale variations are primarily concentrated at ~30 km (as determined from spectral analyses, not shown). Interestingly, the along-slope bottom topography also exhibits a spectral peak at ~30 km suggesting that the short-wavelength fluctuations might be internal waves generated by flow over the topography, although inertial waves and/or eddies might also contribute to the small scale fluctuations. The vertical excursions of the isopycnals associated with these smaller scale fluctuations are about 10 – 15 m as estimated from neighboring XCTD profiles similar to those shown in **Figure 1**. The larger scale mode of variability is associated with the eastward increase in salinity from 32.8 to 33.2 between 159°W to 147°W and suggests that the halocline shoals over this portion of the slope and then deepens to the east.

This large-scale change is also present at greater depths as evident in the along-slope profiles of temperature and salinity (**Figure 36**). Temperatures are between -1.4°C and -1.7°C in the upper 100 m and then increase to ~0°C at 225 m depth near the base of the halocline. The 0°C and -1.0°C isotherms both bow upward by ~25 m over the central portion of the slope and then plunge downwards at the eastern and western ends of the transect. The deeper isotherms are flatter, although there is east-to-west cooling in the warm (~0.5 C) core of the Modified Atlantic water centered at ~400 m.

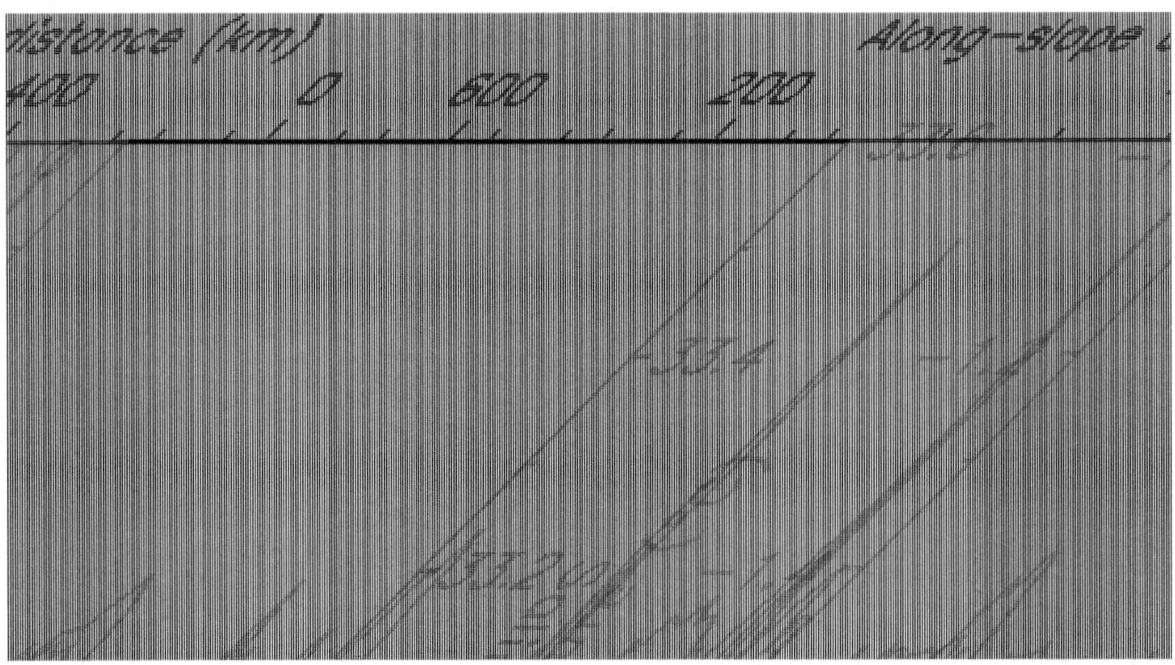

Figure 35: Along-slope temperature (red) and salinity (blue) at 117 m ($\pm$ 1 m) from the temperature/conductivity recorder in the submarine sail, April, 1999.

The salinity section also shows that the 32 isohaline shoals between the western and central portions of the section (in agreement with the submarine sail data) and the 33 and 34.5 isohalines bow upwards in the central Beaufort, similar to the isotherms at ~200 m deep. Thus, the along-slope structure of the halocline is that of an inverted bowl with the halocline depth at the western and eastern edges of the bowl ~25 m deeper than the inverted base of the bowl over the central slope. Later we argue that this structure of the halocline has important implications for the dynamics of the slope current field. Note also that this large-scale 25 m doming

of the halocline exceeds the range in vertical scales of the halocline fluctuations associated with the small along-slope wavelength eddies and internal waves inferred from the submarine sail data. On this basis we suggest that the coarser scale XCTD sampling is not aliased by these smaller scale features. Changes in the depth of the halocline imply along-slope density and pressure gradients as manifested in the dynamic topography (vertically integrated density anomaly) referenced to either 400 or 900 db (**Figure 37**).

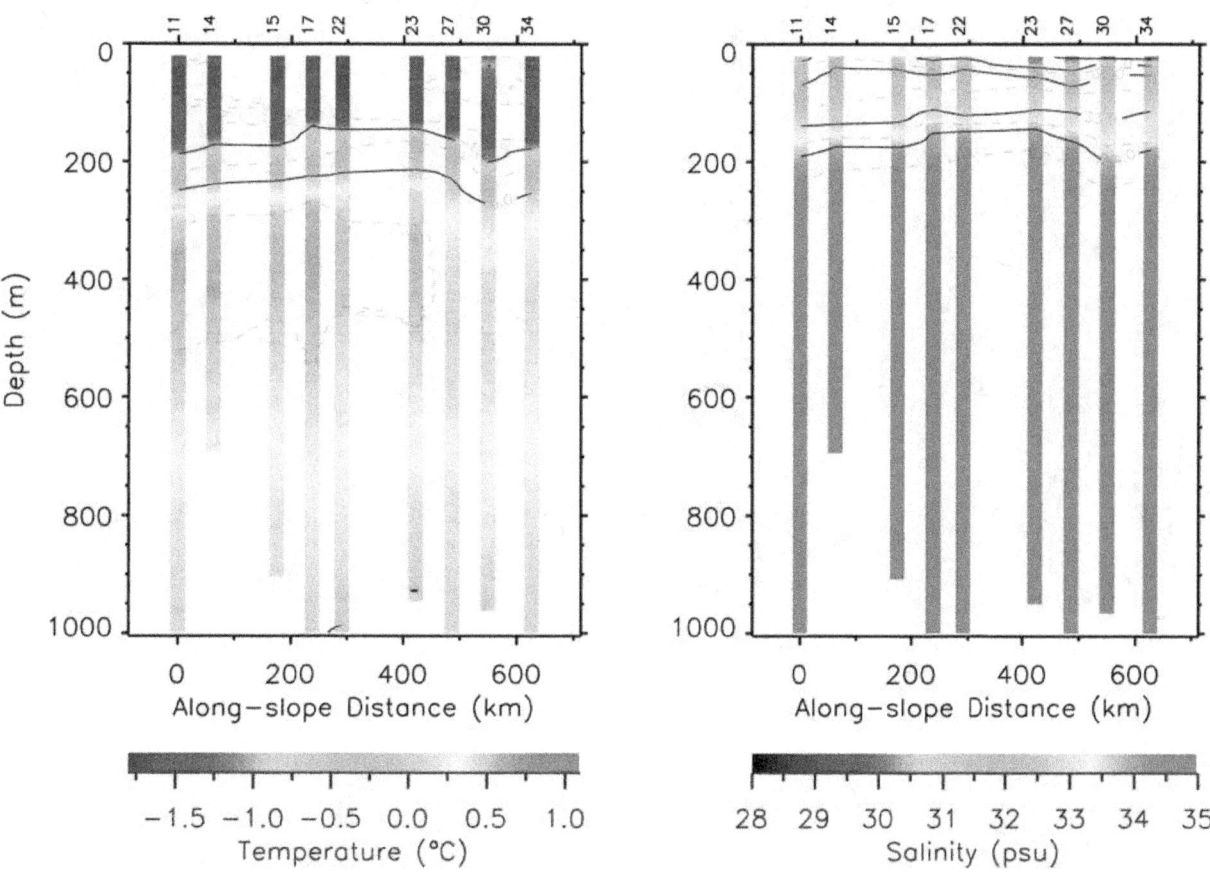

Figure 36: Along-slope section of temperature (left) and salinity (right) based upon the XCTD data. The along-slope XCTD stations are indicated at the top of each figure and their location is shown in **Figure 7**.

The dynamic topography slopes downward from the western to the central Beaufort and then upward to the east at depths above 300 m. At greater depths the dynamic topography is nearly flat. This indicates, then, that the pressure gradient is largely associated with changes in the depth of the halocline *and* in changes in the density of the polar mixed layer, but not with deeper along-slope density variations. If, to lowest order, the cross-slope flow is in geostrophic balance then there is a southward cross-slope geostrophic flow in the western Beaufort Sea and a northward cross-slope geostrophic flow in the eastern Beaufort Sea. These cross-slope flows are weak, however, having a magnitude of ~1 cm s^{-1} above 250 m depth, which is consistent with the weak cross-slope velocities measured by the current meters.

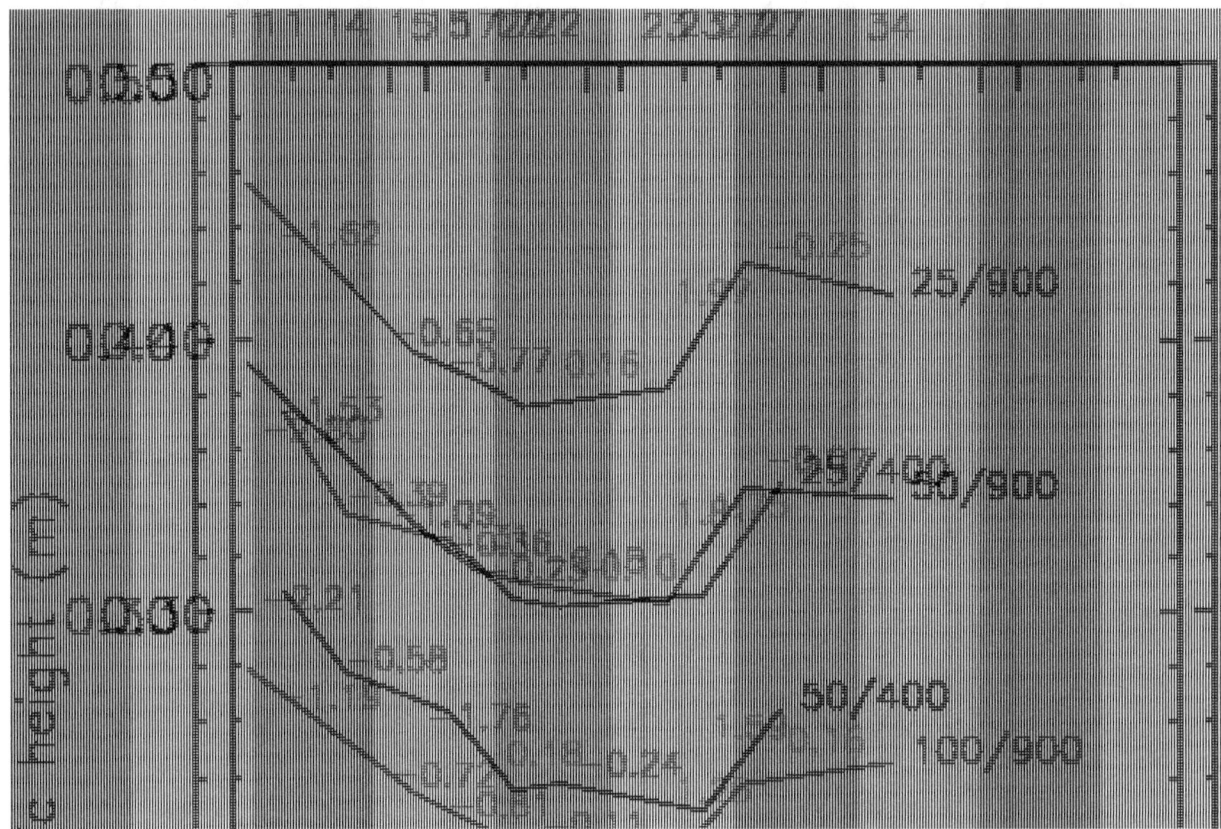

Figure 37: Along-slope dynamic topography referenced to a) 400 db and b) 900 db based on the along-slope XCTD stations indicated at the top of each figure. The location of these stations is shown in Figure 7. Blue (negative) numbers indicate southward geostrophic flow and red (positive) numbers indicate northward geostrophic flow. Velocity units are cm s^{-1}.

IV.7 Beaufort Slope Dynamics

Figure 38 is a map of record-length mean currents ~50 m depth (for the Chukchi Sea) and at ~100m depth (along the Beaufort slope). We have chosen the 100 m depth as being most closely representative of the flow at the shelfbreak. The Chukchi measurements are from *Weingartner et al.* [accepted] and *Woodgate et al.* [accepted] and span the period 1990–1995. The Beaufort slope measurements from this report are combined with the current measurements made in 1986 – 87 by *Aagaard et al.* [1986]. Mean currents along the Mackenzie continental slope are from *Kulikov et al.* [1998].

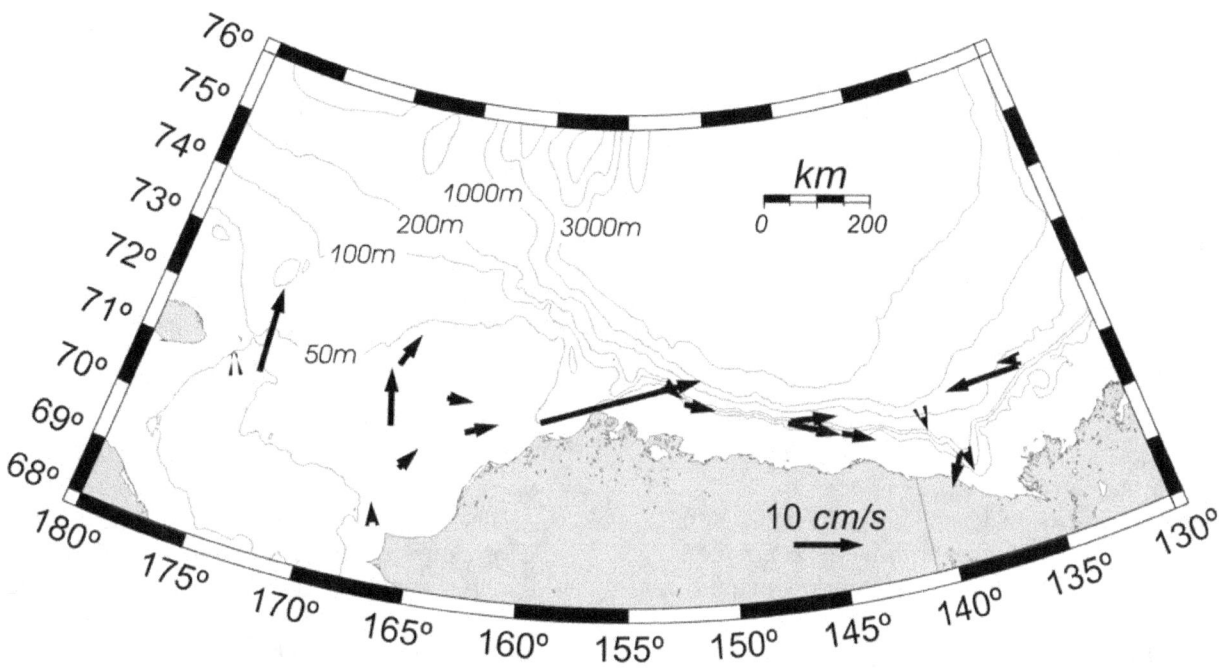

Figure 38: Composite map of mean currents over the Chukchi shelf and Beaufort slope. Only current vectors from ~100 m depth have been used in constructing this figure.

Although made in different years, in aggregate, the results suggest that waters flowing from the Chukchi shelf contribute to the eastward (subsurface) flow along the Alaskan Beaufort slope at least as far east as 144°W. Some caution is required in interpreting the flows in the eastern Beaufort (B5) and from *Kulikov et al.*, however. For example, B5 might not be a good representation of the shelfbreak flow since it is further seaward of the shelfbreak (owing to the broadening of the continental slope) than the measurements to the west. Moreover, *Kulikov et al.*'s measurements near the Mackenzie Canyon might suffer from local topographic effects associated with the mouth of this canyon. Finally, their measurements along the Mackenzie slope (~135°W) are only from summer, although they find that the flow here is consistently steady and westward. While there is some question on how representative some of the measurements are of the eastern (and Mackenzie) Beaufort slope, the observed currents, when combined with the hydrography, raise critical questions pertaining to the along-

slope continuity of the undercurrent, and in particular, the extent to which it continues eastward into the Mackenzie Beaufort shelfbreak and slope.

In spite of the considerable spatial and temporal variability in the along-slope density field our results suggest that the along-slope variation in the vertical displacement of the halocline along the Chukchi-Beaufort slope is that of an inverted bowl, with the halocline shallow along the central Beaufort slope and deeper to the east and west. *Csanady* [1985] examined theoretically the steady shelfbreak flow fields associated with just such an along-slope pycnocline structure and uniform along-slope bathymetry. His solution for the steady flow field (with wind stress neglected) is similar to that described based on the submarine hydrography and consists of: 1) onshore geostrophic flow along the eastern Chukchi/western Beaufort slope, 2) offshore geostrophic flow in the eastern Beaufort, and 3) along-slope eastward flow at the shelfbreak that connects the two regions. For this case, the result suggests that undercurrent waters are carried offshore where the halocline deepens in the eastern Beaufort Sea. Moreover, *Csanady's* solution indicates a weak westward flow at the shelfbreak in the eastern Beaufort Sea. *Hill* [1995] examined the response of a steady along-slope barotropic current over a continental slope which broadens in the direction of the flow and finds that the current also broadens as it flows downstream. Both theoretical results are consistent with the suggestion that the undercurrent weakens as it enters the eastern Beaufort Sea.

Adding an opposing along-slope surface wind stress to the along-slope density gradient will alter the vertical structure of the flow, but not necessarily change the basic dynamics of the undercurrent. For a westward wind stress the near surface flow will be westward, with the westward flow diminishing with depth and reversing where the along-slope pressure gradient exceeds the stress. The eastward flow is eventually balanced by bottom stress so that at steady state a vertically sheared flow develops that is westward at the surface and eastward at depth. We consider this to be the lowest order along-slope momentum balance over the Beaufort slope. Quite possibly along-slope advection of eastward momentum is important in the momentum balance in the western Beaufort Sea, for it appears from preliminary calculations that this term is about the same magnitude as the vertically integrated wind stress. In contrast, vertical advection of eastward momentum appears to be an order of magnitude smaller on average.

Since the along-slope density field appears crucial to the eastward flow of the undercurrent along the Beaufort slope, it must be maintained against the eroding influence of both advection and diffusion. For the western Beaufort Sea we suggest that the density gradient is maintained by the (more or less steady) outflow of moderately saline Pacific waters from the Chukchi shelf. These primarily affect the upper 150 m of the slope. This pool of moderately saline water is continually replenished by the outflow from the Chukchi Sea shelf. There is no comparable source of moderately saline water that feeds the upper halocline along the Alaskan

Beaufort shelf. Moreover, it is conceivable that the upwelling response to westward winds is greater over the central Beaufort, where shelf outflows are absent, than over the western Beaufort and Chukchi continental slopes. Such a response would further enhance the along-slope density gradient between the western and central Beaufort slope.

The reversal in sign of the along-slope density gradient might be related to outflows from the Mackenzie shelf. The density of this outflow varies seasonally and is large and fresh in summer due to the massive Mackenzie River discharge at this time and by modest salinization of the discharge in the flaw lead system that forms in winter over this shelf [*Melling*, 1993; *MacDonald and Carmack, 1991*]. If these outflows pool along the Mackenzie continental slope, they could effect a reversal in the sign of the along-slope density gradient and force a westward flow. This hypothesis is consistent with the current observations of [*Kulikov et al., 1998*] shown in **Figure 38**. They found a mean westward flow at 133 m of ~10 cm s^{-1} in a water depth of 200 m along the bathymetrically smooth Mackenzie shelf break (134.5°W) during spring and summer 1987. They also find a mean westward flow of ~4 cm s^{-1} at the mouth of Mackenzie Canyon (~138.5°W) in a water depth of 200 m for the period March 1987 – March 1988. We emphasize, however, that these conclusions are tentative for the reasons cited earlier. Moreover, there is little long-term information from this region so that the measurements described herein might be an indication of interannual variability and not an indicator of mean conditions. If, in fact, the slope flows are convergent in the vicinity of the Canada-U.S. EEZ boundary, then both shelfbreak currents turn offshore, most probably decomposing into eddies that propagate into the interior.

On a broader scale our results raise questions regarding the pathway that Pacific waters follow to Fram Strait, where they are returned to the North Atlantic Ocean. Pacific waters appear to leave the Arctic Ocean via an eastward flow along the north Greenland continental slope [*Newton and Sotirin*, 1997]. It was presumed that this flow represented an extension of the Beaufort undercurrent, which continued around the margin of the Canada Basin. Our findings call into question this premise.

If a large along-slope density gradient is a persistent feature of the Beaufort continental slope, it is unlikely to influence the nearshore circulation because, as *Csanady's* [1985] results demonstrate, the along-slope pressure gradient is attenuated inshore of the shelfbreak, with the shelfbreak effectively insulating the nearshore from the slope dynamics. This is not inconsistent with the results from *Weingartner et al.* [2005] who found that there was no mean along-slope pressure gradient on the inner Beaufort Sea shelf. Nevertheless, the question remains how far inshore the slope pressure field might extend. This cannot be addressed with our data, although our hypothesis that the along-slope dynamic topography gradient is established by outflows of relatively low density water from the Chukchi and Mackenzie shelves does have implications for the Alaskan Beaufort continental shelf. It would appear likely that these outflows would result in along-shelf density gradients over the Beaufort Sea shelf. Most likely this gradient will be largest in the western Beaufort Sea due to the persistent discharge from the Mackenzie River compared to the small (in summer) or negligible (in winter) river discharge onto the Alaskan Beaufort Sea. While we suspect that most of the canyon outflow is constrained by the canyon's topography to continue to the shelfbreak before turning eastward, some should also flow eastward over the shelf. Very likely the density difference between Beaufort and Chukchi shelf water is not that large (especially in winter) so that the along-shelf density gradient could be small. Nevertheless, if these gradients exist they could be an important element in the dynamics of the Beaufort Sea shelf, for they would tend to drive a mean cross-slope flow whose magnitude is proportional to the strength of the density gradient. For example, in the eastern Beaufort Sea the low density water associated with Mackenzie shelf water would tend to force an offshore flow over the shelf.

V. Summary and Recommendations

1. The mean monthly along-slope component of the winds was eastward in all months except January 1999, when winds were weakly westward. The monthly wind variance shows no seasonal variation in contrast to climatology, which indicates a doubling in variance from summer to winter.

2. The mean subsurface flow, at depths between 80 and 200 meters, is eastward along the western and central Beaufort slope. This flow frequently reverses, with reversals accompanied by upwelling, but there is no distinct seasonal signal in the shelfbreak flow. This finding contrasts with the large seasonal signal in transport in Bering Strait and over the Chukchi shelf

3. The spatial coherence of the flow field suggests an along-slope decorrelation scale of at least 200 km between the western and central Beaufort shelfbreak. However, along-slope current variations were virtually incoherent between the central and western Beaufort Sea. The cross-slope correlation structure suggests that the slope flow field has a complicated structure, which was not adequately resolved by the sampling design and equipment failures. The decorrelation scale between the central and eastern Beaufort Sea is smaller, but could not be determined from this study.

4. The coherence between winds and along-slope currents varies as a function of depth and distance seaward of the shelfbreak. The largest correlations occur for upper level currents ($\leq\sim$100 m depth) in the western and central Beaufort Sea. Deeper currents and currents in the eastern Beaufort showed little or no coherence with the winds. The low coherence might be explicable in terms of seasonal variation in the sea ice distribution. It appears that during the winter of 1999, the pack ice was immobile for extensive periods of time in the eastern Beaufort Sea. This implies that little of the surface wind stress is transmitted into the water column, hence the wind-current correlation might be weak due to seasonal and shorter period variations in the ice-water stress. However, in conjunction with conclusion 3, the results suggest that the slope flow is largely influenced by the deep ocean and/or by remotely forced topographic waves.

5. Our results, along with measurements made along the Mackenzie Beaufort slope, suggest that the eastward-flowing Beaufort undercurrent might not extend beyond the eastern portion of the Alaskan Beaufort slope. Instead, the current measurements and hydrography indicate that the eastern Alaskan Beaufort slope might be one of along-slope convergence, wherein the eastward flow in the undercurrent meets the westward flow along the Mackenzie shelfbreak. The merged flows are likely diverted offshore in the form of eddies.

6. We emphasize that the eastern Beaufort mooring may not be representative of conditions at the shelfbreak because the continental slope broadens from west to east. Consequently, this mooring was further seaward of the shelfbreak than the moorings to the west. Very likely we have missed important shelfbreak processes in this region and this caveat must be borne in mind when considering the above conclusions.

7. We hypothesize that there is a substantial along-slope density gradient in the vicinity of the Canada/U.S. EEZ line and that this gradient extends across the shelf. The existence of such a gradient has important implications for both the cross- and along-shelf flow structure in this region.

Future measurements in this region should address the following issues:

1. There are no data upon which to test the hypothesis advanced in point #7. An effort should be made to assess the along-shelf/slope density gradients from synoptic scale measurements made at high horizontal and vertical resolution. This could involve CTD casts and/or continuously recording, towed instrument packages.

2. The measurements obtained in this program were unable to assess the onshelf extent to which shelfbreak and slope processes extend. This has been a problem because of the risk to mooring integrity by

deep ice keels in relatively shallow water. However, the use of near-bottom ADCPs, such as those employed on the inner shelf by *Weingartner et al.* [2005], considerably reduce the risks entailed in undertaking such measurements.

3. Nor were we able to provide estimates of the transport along the continental slope and how this transport changes between the western and eastern Beaufort Sea. This is a key set of measurements that will help diagnose the regional flow dynamics and serve as an important comparison for regional circulation models that may be used in establishing oil spill risk assessments.

4. Future shelfbreak and slope current measurements need to incorporate ADCP technology and moored profiling CTDs because these instruments can resolve the complex vertical structure of the flow field, including the uppermost 20 m. Such moorings have recently been used with great success in the western Beaufort Sea by R. Pickart (pers. comm.) as part of the NSF and ONR sponsored Shelf-Basin Interaction in the Western Arctic Program.

VI. References

Aagaard, K. 1984. The Beaufort undercurrent, p. 47–71. *In* P. Barnes and E. Reimnitz [eds.], The Alaskan Beaufort Sea: Ecosystems and Environment. Academic Press, New York.

Aagaard, K. 1989. A synthesis of the Arctic Ocean circulation. Rapp. P.-V. Reun. Cons. Int. Explor. Mer 188:11–22.

Aagaard, K., and E.C. Carmack. 1994. The Arctic Ocean and climate: A perspective, p. 5–20. *In* O.M. Johannessen, R.D. Muench and J.E. Overland [eds.], The Polar Oceans and Their Role in Shaping Global Environment: The Nansen Centennial Volume. American Geophysical Union, Washington, D.C.

Aagaard, K., L.K. Coachman and E. Carmack. 1981. On the halocline of the Arctic Ocean. Deep Sea Res. Part A 28(6):529–545. doi: 10.1016/0198-0149(81)90115-1

Aagaard, K., C.H. Pease, A.T. Roach and S.A. Salo. 1989. Beaufort Sea Mesoscale Circulation Study – Final Report. NOAA Tech. Memo. ERL-PMEL-90. Pacific Marine Environmental Laboratory, Seattle, 114 p.

Carmack, E.C. 1986. Circulation and mixing in ice-covered waters, p. 641–712. *In* N. Untersteiner [ed.], The Geophysics of Sea Ice. NATO ASI Series. Series B, Physics, Vol. 146. Plenum Press, New York.

Coachman, L.K., and C.A. Barnes. 1962. Surface water in the Eurasian Basin of the Arctic Ocean. Arctic 15(4):251–277.

Csanady, G.T. 1985. "Pycnobathic" currents over the upper continental slope. J. Phys. Oceanogr. 15(3):306–315. doi: 10.1175/1520-0485(1985)015<0306:COTUCS>2.0.CO;2

Furey, P.W. 1996. The large-scale surface wind field over the western Arctic Ocean, 1981–1993. M.S. Thesis, Univ. Alaska Fairbanks, 121 p.

Gawarkiewicz, G. 2000. Effects of ambient stratification and shelfbreak topography on offshore transport of dense water on continental shelves. J. Geophys. Res. 105(C2):3307–3324. doi: 10.1029/1999JC900298

Guay, C.K., and K.K. Falkner. 1997. Barium as a tracer of Arctic halocline and river waters. Deep Sea Res. Part II 44(8):1543–1569. doi: 10.1016/S0967-0645(97)00066-0

Haidvogel, D.B., and K.H. Brink. 1986. Mean currents driven by topographic drag over the continental shelf and slope. J. Phys. Oceanogr. 16(12):2159–2171. doi: 10.1175/1520-0485(1986)016<2159:MCDBTD>2.0.CO;2

Hart, J.E., and P.D. Killworth. 1976. On open ocean baroclinic instability in the Arctic. Deep Sea Res. Oceanogr. Abstr. 23(7):637–645. doi: 10.1016/0011-7471(76)90006-1

Hill, A.E. 1995. Leakage of barotropic slope currents onto the continental shelf. J. Phys. Oceanogr. 25(7):1617–1621. doi: 10.1175/1520-0485(1995)025<1617:LOBSCO>2.0.CO;2

Holloway, G. 1992. Representing topographic stress for large-scale ocean models. J. Phys. Oceanogr. 22(9):1033–1046. doi: 10.1175/1520-0485(1992)022<1033:RTSFLS>2.0.CO;2

Huthnance, J.M. 1984. Slope currents and "JEBAR". J. Phys. Oceanogr. 14(4):795–810. doi: 10.1175/1520-0485(1984)014<0795:SCA>2.0.CO;2

Huthnance, J.M. 1995. Circulation, exchange and water masses at the ocean margin: The role of physical processes at the shelf edge. Prog. Oceanogr. 35(4):353–431. doi: 10.1016/0079-6611(95)80003-C

Jones, E.P., and L.G. Anderson. 1986. On the origin of the chemical properties of the Arctic Ocean halocline. J. Geophys. Res. 91(C9):10759–10767.

Kundu, P.K., and J.P. McCreary, Jr. 1986. On the dynamics of the throughflow from the Pacific into the Indian Ocean. J. Phys. Oceanogr. 16(12):2191–2198. doi: 10.1175/1520-0485(1986)016<2191:OTDOTT>2.0.CO;2

Macdonald, R.W., and E.C. Carmack. 1991. The role of large-scale under-ice topography in separating estuary and ocean on an Arctic shelf. Atmos.-Ocean 29(1):37–53.

Macdonald, R.W., E.C. Carmack, F.A. McLaughlin, K.K. Falkner and J.H. Swift. 1999. Connections among ice, runoff, and atmospheric forcing in the Beaufort Gyre. Geophys. Res. Lett. 26(15):2223–2226. doi: 10.1029/1999GL900508

Macdonald, R.W., E.C. Carmack, F.A. McLaughlin, K. Iseki, D.M. Macdonald and M.C. O'Brien. 1989. Composition and modification of water masses in the Mackenzie shelf estuary. J. Geophys. Res. 94(C12):18057–18070. doi: 10.1029/89JC03033

Manley, T.O., and K. Hunkins. 1985. Mesoscale eddies of the Arctic Ocean. J. Geophys. Res. 90(C3):4911–4930.

McCreary, J.P., Jr. 1981. A linear stratified ocean model of the coastal undercurrent. Phil. Trans. R. Soc. Lond. A 302(1469):385–413. http://links.jstor.org/sici?sici=0080-4614%2819810924%29302%3A1469%3C385%3AALSOMO%3E2.0.CO%3B2-A

McLaughlin, F.A., E.C. Carmack, R.W. Macdonald, H. Melling, J.H. Swift, P.A. Wheeler, B.F. Sherr and E.B. Sherr. 2004. The joint roles of Pacific and Atlantic-origin waters in the Canada Basin, 1997–1998. Deep-Sea Res. Part I 51(1):107–128. doi: 10.1016/j.dsr.2003.09.010

McLaughlin, F., E. Carmack, R. Macdonald, A.J. Weaver and J. Smith. 2002. The Canada Basin, 1989–1995: Upstream events and far-field effects of the Barents Sea. J. Geophys. Res. 107(C7):10129–10149. doi:10.1029/2001JC000904

Melling, H. 1993. The formation of a haline shelf front in wintertime in an ice-covered arctic sea. Cont. Shelf Res. 13(10):1123–1147. doi: 10.1016/0278-4343(93)90045-Y

Melling, H., and R.M. Moore. 1995. Modification of halocline source waters during freezing on the Beaufort Sea shelf: Evidence from oxygen isotopes and dissolved nutrients. Cont. Shelf Res. 15(1):89–113. doi: 10.1016/0278-4343(94)P1814-R

Muench, R.D., J.T. Gunn, T.E. Whitledge, P. Schlosser and W. Smethie, Jr. 2000. An Arctic Ocean cold core eddy. J. Geophys. Res. 105(C10):23997–24006. doi: 10.1029/2000JC000212

Newton, J.L., K. Aagaard and L.K. Coachman. 1974. Baroclinic eddies in the Arctic Ocean. Deep Sea Res. Oceanogr. Abstr. 21(9):707–719. doi: 10.1016/0011-7471(74)90078-3

Newton, J.L., and B.J. Sotirin. 1997. Boundary undercurrent and water mass changes in the Lincoln Sea. J. Geophys. Res. 102(C2):3393–3404. doi: 10.1029/96JC03441

North, G.R., T.L. Bell and R.F. Cahalan. 1982. Sampling errors in the estimation of empirical orthogonal functions. Mon. Weather Rev. 110(7):699–706.

Philander, S.G.H., and J.-H. Yoon. 1982. Eastern boundary currents and coastal upwelling. J. Phys. Oceanogr. 12(8):862–879. doi: 10.1175/1520-0485(1982)012<0862:EBCACU>2.0.CO;2

Pickart, R.S. 2004. Shelfbreak circulation in the Alaskan Beaufort Sea: Mean structure and variability. J. Geophys. Res. 109(C04024). doi: 0.1029/2003JC001912

Pickart, R.S., T.J. Weingartner, L.J. Pratt, S. Zimmermann and D.J. Torres. 2005. Flow of winter-transformed Pacific water into the western Arctic. Deep-Sea Res. Part II 52(24–26):3175–3198. doi: 10.1016/j.dsr2.2005.10.009

Ponte, R.M. 1995. Viscid eastern boundary dynamics and the spreading of Mediterranean Water along the Portuguese continental slope. J. Phys. Oceanogr. 25(1):2437–2443. doi: 10.1175/1520-0485(1995)025<2437:VEBDAT>2.0.CO;2

Rudels, B., E.P. Jones, L.G. Anderson and G. Kattner. 1994. On the intermediate depth waters of the Arctic Ocean, p. 33–46. *In* O.M. Johannessen, R.D. Muench and J.E. Overland [eds.], The Polar Oceans and Their Role in Shaping Global Environment: The Nansen Centennial Volume. American Geophysical Union, Washington, D.C.

Schauer, U., R.D. Muench, B. Rudels and L. Timokhov. 1997. Impact of eastern Arctic shelf waters on the Nansen Basin intermediate layers. J. Geophys. Res. 102(C2):3371–3338. doi: 10.1029/96JC03366

Shimada, K., E.C. Carmack, K. Hatakeyama and T. Takizawa. 2001. Varieties of shallow temperature maximum waters in the western Canadian Basin of the Arctic Ocean. Geophys. Res. Lett. 28(18):3441–3444. doi: 10.1029/2001GL013168

Steele, M., J.H. Morison and T.B. Curtin. 1995. Halocline water formation in the Barents Sea. J. Geophys. Res. 100(C1):881–894. doi: 10.1029/94JC02310

Weingartner, T., K. Aagaard, R. Woodgate, S. Danielson, Y. Sasaki and D. Cavalieri. 2005. Circulation on the north central Chukchi Sea Shelf. Deep-Sea Res. Part II 52(24–26):3150–3174. doi: 10.1016/j.dsr2.2005.10.015

Weingartner, T.J., D.J. Cavalieri, K. Aagaard and Y. Sasaki. 1998. Circulation, dense water formation, and outflow on the northeast Chukchi shelf. J. Geophys. Res. 103(C4):7647–7661. doi: 10.1029/98JC00374

Woodgate, R.A., K. Aagaard, R.D. Muench, J. Gunn, G. Björk, B. Rudels, A.T. Roach and U. Schauer. 2001. The Arctic Ocean boundary current along the Eurasian slope and the adjacent Lomonosov Ridge: Water mass properties, transports and transformations from moored instruments. Deep Sea Res. Part I 48(8):1757–1792. doi: 10.1016/S0967-0637(00)00091-1

Woodgate, R.A., K. Aagaard and T.J. Weingartner. 2005. A year in the physical oceanography of the Chukchi Sea: Moored measurements from autumn 1990–91. Deep-Sea Res. Part II 52(24–26):3116–3149. doi: 10.1016/j.dsr2.2005.10.016